The Breakfast Cookbook

"From Your Hungry Husband"

The
Breakfast
Cookbook

CEIL DYER

AN ESSANDESS SPECIAL EDITION

NEW YORK 1968

Contents

Introduction

Breakfast is such an emotional meal—really, there's no other way to describe it.

Many's the man who will eat indifferent food each night of the week and never complain, yet who will howl with rage if his morning eggs are not cooked exactly three minutes. Many's the girl who, caring not one bit "what's for lunch," will send back her coffee time and time again because it's too strong, too weak, too hot, or too—something.

There are some people who won't start the day without orange juice, and others who consider grapefruit a morning must. Some people refuse to eat eggs at all unless they're scrambled, while their best friends insist on eggs sunny-side-up—but only with home fries, please.

Fried fish for breakfast? "What a delicacy," says the gourmet. "How awful," answers his spouse. "Give me cereal with fresh fruit and milk or I simply will not get up." Omelets, not porridge; flapjacks, not crêpes; tea with lemon—no, coffee with cream. . . . We could go on forever; there are so many conflicting ideas. To say the least, the break-the-fast meal provokes controversy, and what's more, it always has.

Breakfast, as we know it, dates from the introduction of coffee and tea in Europe. Coffee, which was popularized in France by the Turkish ambassador to the court of Louis XIV, probably first appeared in England during Cromwell's time. Tea came to England by way of Asia. It is said to have been introduced by Lord Arlington in the year 1666. Clergymen and doctors roundly denounced both beverages as "demoralizing" and "very bad for the health." Nonetheless, they gradually won public acceptance, though men continued to drink ale, wine, or spirits of some sort long after their wives had abandoned such "crudities" for the more refined and elegant beverages.

The English took to tea, the French adopted coffee, and each group proclaimed the virtues of his particular cup. The best morning beverage? Why the subject raises heat even today, and we doubt if the issue will ever be resolved.

It is coffee, however, that is America's most popular morning brew. The original choice was more a matter of politics than of taste preference. Tea was once the favored drink, but after it was taxed by the British, Colonial housewives simply refused to pay the resulting high prices. Remember "no taxation without representation," the Boston Tea Party, and— but then you know the historical facts. Except for the beverage, however, today's typical American breakfast is basically English in origin. And we should be grateful that our English cousins were so quick to appreciate the advantages of a nourishing start to the day.

What is an average American breakfast? Ask, and you'll probably be told, "Why it's juice, bacon and eggs, toast, and coffee." But inquire as to how it should be prepared, and the breakfast controversy starts anew. Undoubtedly, breakfast offers more possibilities for individual preference than any other repast. It is the meal at which the greatest number of dishes can be served in the greatest number of ways. What constitutes a good breakfast to one man, though, is something else entirely to his wife. There appears to be agreement on only one thing: a good breakfast is essential to well-being and health.

We ask your pardon, then, if our own preferences intrude now and then in the following chapters. We have tried to be impartial, but it was so difficult to slight any of our own morning favorites. However, our menus are designed to suggest, not to direct. Each may be altered to suit the season, the hour of the meal, your own taste and appetite, and those of your guests. Menus range from a quick and easy family meal to a wedding breakfast deluxe; from a breakfast à deux, for just you and your spouse, to a party brunch to serve at 2 A.M. after a night on the town.

As to our recipes, our aim is quite simple. We mean to inspire. Included are traditional mainstays—griddle cakes and bacon, eggs and corned beef hash—and out-of-the-ordinary dishes such as kedgeree and crêpes with delicate fillings. Easy-to-follow instructions enable you to prepare all breakfast foods in gourmet fashion.

And although you may be surprised at the inclusion of dishes you've never considered breakfast fare, we hope that you will find the ideas tempting enough to try. Breakfast is a necessity, but it is not necessary to have the same breakfast prepared in the same way day after day. Our book is full of simple innovations—new ways to prepare eggs, pancakes, breads, and beverages which can be adapted to your own tastes. With a little pre-planning, breakfast can be the easiest as well as the most interesting meal to assemble.

For a perfect breakfast every day, arrange a colorful table setting. A set of gay pottery dishes or flower-sprigged china will create a cheerful decor. Be sure to have enough proper cooking equipment, such as omelet pans, soufflé dishes, and ramekins for quick-to-fix eggs. These are handy utensils for party buffets, too. For pure luxury, buy an electric squeezer or blender for fresh fruit treats. A good coffeepot is probably your best investment—it makes "the making" worth the effort. Most important, vary your menus whether you're planning a quick or a leisurely breakfast.

You can begin each day with a new breakfast adventure. The most important meal of the day offers the most possibilities for pleasure.

Juices and Fruits
plus
Pre-Breakfast Drinks

You don't really need a recipe for the morning's first fruit or juice; freshly squeezed or sliced, fruit is pure perfection. However, even the simplest meal takes on a festive air when the fruit is made interesting, so why not indulge? The cost is no more, and there's little or no work in the preparing.

Here's an assortment of ways to bring raves from those who partake: chilled juices, fruit combinations, and cooked fruits, plus a few, just a few, high-spirited drinks that are meant only for light pre-brunch imbibing.

Light and frothy, these quick-and-easy concoctions are for blender fans. You can improvise with whatever fresh and canned fruits and vegetables you have on hand.
Put all ingredients except ice in the blender, and blend until they are liquefied. Add crushed ice, blend until smooth, and serve in chilled glasses.

Each recipe is for 2 large or 4 small servings.

APPLE FRAPPÉ

    ¾ cup apple juice (canned or bottled)
    1 tablespoon lemon juice
    2 teaspoons sugar
    1 apple, pared, cored, and cut into cubes
    ½ cup crushed ice

ORANGE APRICOT FRAPPÉ

    1½ cups fresh orange juice
    1½ cups stewed apricots
    1 teaspoon lemon juice
    sugar to taste
    ½ cup crushed ice

ORANGE CANTALOUPE FRAPPÉ

    1 cup cantaloupe, peeled, seeded, and diced
    2 cups fresh orange juice
    ½ cup crushed ice

TOMATO AND CUCUMBER COCKTAIL

    ½ small cucumber, pared and diced
    2 cups tomato juice
    2 teaspoons lemon juice
    dash of Tabasco sauce
    ½ teaspoon salt
    1 cup crushed ice

You don't always have to squeeze oranges, you know. Why not embellish the fruit?

GLORIFIED ORANGES WITH SOUR CREAM
SERVES SIX

    6 large California seedless oranges
    2 tablespoons brown sugar
    1 cup sour cream
    2 tablespoons grated orange peel

Peel and section oranges. Place in serving dish, sprinkle with half the brown sugar. Cover with sour cream. Sprinkle cream with remaining sugar and grated orange peel.

GRAPEFRUIT SHELLS
SERVES TWO

1 grapefruit
2 oranges, peeled and diced
2 teaspoons sugar
1 teaspoon kirsch

Halve the grapefruit and remove the pulp, discarding seeds and membrane. Combine with diced oranges, sprinkle with sugar and kirsch. Pile into grapefruit shells. Chill before serving.

MINTED BAKED APPLES
SERVES SIX

6 baking apples
6 tablespoons sugar
6 teaspoons butter
½ cup hot water
3 tablespoons mint jelly

Core the apples, peel the upper half from each, and place in baking dish. Fill each core with 1 teaspoon sugar and 1 teaspoon butter. Mix hot water with mint jelly, pour around apples. Bake at 350°F. until tender (35 to 45 minutes). Baste frequently. Transfer apples to serving dish, reduce liquid in pan to half, and pour over apples. Serve at room temperature.

POACHED APPLES
SERVES FOUR TO SIX

2 pounds crisp apples
3 tablespoons butter
¾ cup sugar
1 cup apple cider
peel from ½ lemon, cut in thin slices (all white
    membrane removed)

Peel, core, and cut apples into thick wedges. Sauté in butter
in heavy skillet for 2 to 3 minutes. Add sugar, apple cider,
and lemon peel. Cover and cook until apples are tender.
Chill in sauce. Serve plain or with cream.

MAPLE SYRUP PEARS
SERVES FOUR TO SIX

6 to 8 pears, peeled, cored, and cut in quarters
1 cup maple syrup
½ cup orange juice
juice from ½ small lemon
rind from ½ orange, cut into julienne strips (all
    white removed)
chopped fresh mint

Combine all ingredients, except mint, in saucepan. Bring to
boil, reduce heat, simmer gently 10 minutes. Cool, pour into
glass serving bowl. Refrigerate until well chilled. Sprinkle
with mint just before serving.

*We delight in frozen foods—especially when frozen fruit is
combined with fresh.*

GINGERED CANTALOUPE
BALLS À L'ORANGE
SERVES FOUR

    ½ can orange juice concentrate, slightly thawed
    4 tablespoons sugar
    4 cups fresh cantaloupe balls
    2 tablespoons chopped candied ginger

Combine orange juice concentrate and sugar; add melon balls. Sprinkle with ginger. Serve at once.

PEACHES WITH
STRAWBERRY PURÉE
SERVES SIX

    8 ripe peaches
    1 package frozen strawberries
    1 tablespoon sugar
    juice from ½ orange

Plunge peaches into boiling water, rinse under cold water, and slip off skins. Cut in half, remove stones, and place in serving bowl. Cut block of frozen strawberries into small pieces. Place in electric blender with sugar and orange juice. Blend until smooth, pour over peaches, and serve.

Fruits add flavor and dash when served with the meal.

GRILLED PINEAPPLE
SERVES FOUR

    8 slices canned pineapple
    ¼ cup brown sugar
    2 tablespoons butter

Place pineapple in shallow baking dish. Sprinkle with brown sugar, dot with butter. Broil under medium flame until thoroughly heated.

SAUTÉED BANANAS
SERVES FOUR

 4 large ripe bananas
 2 tablespoons butter
 2 tablespoons sugar

Peel bananas and cut in half lengthwise. Sauté in butter for 2 or 3 minutes. Add the sugar, cover pan, and cook until sugar has melted and bananas are soft but not mushy.

BAKED PEACHES SUPREME
SERVES SIX

 6 large fresh freestone peaches
 2 tablespoons brown sugar
 2 tablespoons butter
 3 teaspoons cream

Wash and cut peaches in half, sprinkle with brown sugar, and dot with butter. Place them in a shallow pan and bake at 400°F. for 15 minutes. Cover each half with cream. Place under broiler until browned and bubbly.

Tomatoes are marvelous company for fried fish, omelets, soufflés, or bacon and eggs.

BAKED TOMATOES
SERVES FOUR

    4 ripe tomatoes
    2 tablespoons butter
    1 tablespoon minced onions
    ½ cup bread crumbs
    1 teaspoon salt

Wash and cut tomatoes in half. Place in shallow baking dish. Bake at 350°F. for 10 minutes. Melt butter and stir in onion, bread crumbs, and salt. Cover surface of each tomato with this mixture. Return to oven to bake a final 10 minutes or until tomatoes are soft but not mushy.

PARSLEY FRIED
TOMATO SLICES
SERVES FOUR

    2 large ripe tomatoes
    2 tablespoons butter
    ¼ cup chopped fresh parsley
    salt to taste

Cut tomatoes into thick slices. Fry in butter over medium heat for 3 to 4 minutes, turning once. Sprinkle with parsley and salt. Cover pan, cook 2 to 3 minutes longer. Serve with pan butter and parsley "poured over."

GRILLED TOMATOES
WITH SOUR CREAM
SERVES EIGHT

    ½ cup sour cream
    ½ cup mayonnaise
    4 large ripe tomatoes
    cayenne pepper

Mix together the sour cream and mayonnaise. Wash and cut tomatoes in half. Cover each with cream mixture. Place on buttered pan. Bake at 350°F. until soft; dust with cayenne pepper.

A well-chilled compote of fruit—fresh, canned, frozen, stewed, or any such combination—in your best crystal bowl looks beautiful on a breakfast buffet. Sweeten with confectioners' sugar and, if it's brunch-time, flavor with a little brandy, kirsch, cassis, or white wine, or with fruit cordials.

Blend and, to let fruit mellow, chill in the refrigerator for 3 to 4 hours before serving.

APPLE COMPOTE
SERVES SIX TO EIGHT

    1 cup dry white wine
    1 cup raisins
    ½ cup cooked prunes
    1½ cups sugar
    1½ cups water
    1 lemon, cut in wedges
    6 Winesap apples

Pour wine over raisins and prunes; let soak 1 hour or longer. Cook sugar, water, and lemon over medium heat until sugar has dissolved. Add apples, raisins, and prunes plus any wine that has not soaked into fruit. Cook until apples are tender. Chill and serve with whipped or plain cream.

FRESH FRUIT COMPOTE
SERVES EIGHT

    1 pint strawberries, hulled
    4 peaches, peeled and sliced
    2 bananas, peeled and sliced

¼ cup blueberries
½ cup water
½ cup sugar
juice from 1 orange
peel from ½ orange, cut into julienne strips (all
    white removed)
¼ cup kirsch (optional)

Place strawberries, peaches, bananas, and blueberries in serving bowl. Combine water, sugar, orange juice, and orange peel in saucepan. Bring to a boil, simmer 5 minutes. Cool. Add kirsch and pour mixture over fruit. Chill thoroughly before serving.

FRESH FRUIT COMPOTE
WITH FROZEN CHAMPAGNE
SERVES TWELVE OR MORE

2 cups water
1 cup sugar
6 to 8 small peaches
6 to 8 small apricots
2 drops red food coloring
2 apples, peeled, cored, and quartered
2 pears, peeled, cored, and quartered
1 cup champagne
2 tablespoons lemon juice
½ cup seedless grapes
2 bananas, peeled and sliced

Combine sugar and water, bring to a boil in heavy saucepan. Reduce heat, let simmer gently. Plunge peaches and apricots into boiling water for 2 to 3 minutes, rinse under cold water, slip off skins, cut in half, and remove stones. Add to simmering syrup. Cook 5 minutes, remove. Add food coloring to syrup, blend, and add apples and pears.* Cook 10 minutes

* Do not peel and cut fruit until ready to use, as it will discolor.

or until just tender. Remove. Place fruit in crystal or other attractive glass serving dish. Cover and refrigerate. Cool syrup, combine with champagne and lemon juice. Pour into refrigerator tray, freeze to mushy stage, pour over fruit in bowl, add grapes and bananas, blend, and serve.

Cocktails for breakfast? "Heavens to Betsy, how shocking!" say the Aunt Agathas of this world. But we know that you know that these blithe spirits are to be served only for a late breakfast or brunch—and then only one. Any more and you'll spoil a good meal.

MILK PUNCH
SERVES TWO

    2 jiggers cognac
    1 egg
    4 heaping teaspoons French vanilla ice cream
    2 cups milk
    grated nutmeg

Place all ingredients except nutmeg in electric blender and blend at high speed until smooth. (Or place in chilled cocktail shaker and shake until smooth.) Pour into chilled mugs, sprinkle with nutmeg. Serve at once.

For vitamin virtue and also for pure pleasure, combine citrus juice with almost any "spirit."

VODKA SCREWDRIVER
FOR EACH SERVING

    1 jigger vodka
    ice cubes
    fresh orange juice

Place vodka in Old-Fashioned glass. Add ice cubes. Fill glass with orange juice, freshly squeezed.

ORANGE BLOSSOM
FOR EACH SERVING

1 jigger dry gin
juice from 1 orange
crushed ice
½ orange slice

Place in cocktail shaker. Shake well, pour into ice-filled Old-Fashioned glass. Garnish with orange slice.
NOTE: This breakfast version contains double the usual quantity of orange juice and is served "on the rocks," a concession to before-noon imbibing.

SCOTCH OLD-FASHIONED
FOR EACH SERVING

½ lemon slice
½ orange slice
1 teaspoon sugar
1 tablespoon water
2 ounces Scotch
ice cubes
1 orange slice
1 fresh cherry

Mull first 4 ingredients in Old-Fashioned glass. Add Scotch. Fill glass with ice cubes. Garnish with orange slice and cherry. Add more water if you insist, but it's better if you simply twirl the ice cubes around a bit and wait a half-minute before sipping.

RUM SOUR
FOR EACH SERVING

>   juice from ½ lemon
>   1 teaspoon sugar
>   2 ounces light rum
>   ½ cup crushed ice
>   1 orange slice

Place all ingredients except orange slice in cocktail shaker. Shake well and strain into glass. Garnish with orange slice.

The real secret to making a true Ramos Gin Fizz is in the shaking. That is what we were told some years ago by a bartender friend at the Old Roosevelt Hotel in New Orleans. "You can't just shake it up a few times and think you have done the job," he cautioned, "because you haven't—you've only just started."

RAMOS GIN FIZZ
FOR EACH SERVING

>   2 teaspoons powdered sugar
>   4 dashes orange-flower water
>   2½ jiggers London dry gin
>   juice from ½ lemon
>   juice from ¼ lime
>   2 tablespoons heavy cream
>   4 tablespoons seltzer water
>   ¾ cup crushed ice
>   1 egg white, well beaten
>   2 sprigs mint (optional)

Mix together the sugar, orange-flower water, gin, and lemon and lime juices. Add the cream, seltzer water, and ice; place in a well-chilled metal shaker. Shake vigorously, add beaten egg white, and shake again. Pour into tall chilled glass, garnish with mint if desired. Serve at once.

MARGARITAS
FOR EACH SERVING

> lime juice
> coarse salt
> crushed ice
> 1 ounce tequila
> dash of Cointreau
> juice from ½ lime

Moisten rim of stemmed cocktail glass with lime juice. Dip in coarse salt. Fill with crushed ice. Pour in tequila, Cointreau, and lime juice. Stir once and serve.

Here are two drinks to serve at the same party, so your guests can take their choice.

BLOODLESS MARY
FOR EACH SERVING

> 3 ounces tomato juice
> 1 ounce clam juice
> juice from ½ lemon
> dash of Tabasco sauce
> 1 teaspoon Worcestershire sauce
> salt and pepper to taste
> dash of celery salt

Shake vigorously and pour over ice into Old-Fashioned glass.

17

BLOODY MARY

FOR EACH SERVING

> 1½ ounces vodka
> 3 ounces tomato juice
> ½ teaspoon Worcestershire sauce
> dash of Tabasco sauce
> ¼ teaspoon sugar
> salt and pepper to taste
> dash of celery salt
> 2 or 3 cubes of ice

Shake vigorously and strain into Old-Fashioned glass.

Champagne is for all gala occasions. It's also for any ordinary occasion you want to make festive.

DIAMOND FIZZ

FOR EACH SERVING

> 1 teaspoon confectioners' sugar
> 1 teaspoon lemon juice
> 1 jigger gin
> crushed ice
> champagne

In tall glass blend sugar, lemon juice, and gin. Half-fill with crushed ice. Fill with champagne.

CHAMPAGNE WITH PEACHES

FOR EACH SERVING

> 1 peach, blanched and peeled*
> champagne

* To blanch peaches, plunge first in boiling water, then in cold. Skins will slip off easily.

18

Place peach in large champagne glass. Fill glass with champagne. Don't forget to provide a spoon for the peach. It's lovely after drinking the "bubbly."

CHAMPAGNE PUNCH
SERVES TEN TO TWELVE

    1 small ripe pineapple
    1 cup fine sugar
    ¼ cup fresh lemon juice
    1 cup cognac
    ¼ cup peach brandy
    block of ice
    3 bottles champagne (one more bottle of champagne may be added if desired)
    fresh peach slices
    mint sprigs

Peel, core, and dice pineapple. Place in bowl. Sprinkle with sugar. Allow to marinate 1 hour at room temperature. Add lemon juice, cognac, and brandy. Blend gently. Allow to stand 8 to 10 hours. When ready to serve, pour mixture over block of ice in large punch bowl. Pour in champagne. Float peach slices and sprigs of mint on surface.

The Perfect Egg

Although the basic ways of cooking an egg—boiling, poaching, scrambling, frying, and baking—can be counted on the fingers of one hand, there are countless variations on these classic themes: Oeufs sur le Plat, Huevos Rancheros, Eggs Benedict, Oeufs au Beurre Noir—but that's only a beginning, just a hint of the list.

Eggs, the simplest and most plentiful of foods, combine superbly with meat or fish, fruits, vegetables, or cheese. Garnished, sauced, or served plain, eggs can be prepared in a new guise each day of the week. With eggs in her kitchen, no cook need ever be at a loss for a different or delectable breakfast main dish.

Here is the epicure's way with eggs.

BAKED EGGS

Butter individual ramekins or a shallow baking dish. Heat until butter is melted. Break in eggs directly, or cover bottom of dish with cooked vegetables, chopped ham, or crumbled bacon, then break in eggs; dot yolk with butter. Cover with sauce if desired. Bake at 325°F. for 8 to 10 minutes or until whites have set.

POACHED EGGS

Fill skillet ¾ full with beef stock, chicken stock, wine, tomato juice, milk, or, if you must, water. Bring to a simmer. Break eggs, and slip one at a time into liquid. Simmer 4 to 5 minutes. Remove with slotted spoon. Trim edges, hold spoon briefly over paper towel to blot out excess moisture, then place on warm toast, split and buttered corn bread squares, hot buttered biscuits, or English muffins.

FRIED EGGS

Break eggs onto plate, slip into melted butter in warm skillet. Sauté over low flame. Baste yolk with pan butter constantly. When whites are almost set, improve the flavor by adding any of the following to pan butter: 1 tablespoon dry sherry, white wine, dry vermouth, or herb vinegar.

SOFT-COOKED EGGS

Take eggs from refrigerator 30 minutes before preparing. They should be at room temperature before cooking or shells will crack. Place in simmering water; time from the moment water starts to simmer once more. For firm whites but still-liquid yolks, boil 2 to 3 minutes, depending on size of eggs. Cook 2 to 3 minutes longer for yolks that will hold their shape.

SCRAMBLED EGGS

Spread soft butter over the bottom of a thick skillet. Heat to sizzling, add eggs. Cook, stirring constantly over medium heat, until just underdone to your taste. Remove from fire. Heat of pan will complete cooking.

OMELETS

As omelets are a subject unto themselves, you will find instructions for preparing them in the next chapter.

But how will you have your eggs this morning—and what in the world will you serve with them?

For your inspiration we present a dozen egg dishes. Try our suggestions for accompaniments or use your imagination, varying your menus to suit your mood and what is in season and available at your market.

CORNED BEEF HASH AND EGGS
SERVES SIX

2 tablespoons butter
1 tablespoon minced onion
1 tablespoon green pepper
2 cans corned beef hash
salt and coarse-ground black pepper to taste
dash of Tabasco sauce
dash of Worcestershire sauce
6 eggs
paprika

Melt the butter in a large skillet. Add the onion and green pepper. Cook, stirring, until vegetables are limp. Add hash. Blend and break up with spatula or fork. Season to taste with salt, pepper, Tabasco, and Worcestershire sauce. Cook, stirring frequently, until thoroughly hot. With the back of a large spoon make 6 depressions; break 1 egg into each. Cover pan and cook over low heat until egg whites have set. Sprinkle surface of eggs with paprika and serve with rye toast and greengage preserves.

EGG À LA KING ON BAKED HAM SLICES
SERVES FOUR

    4 slices baked ham
    butter or bacon fat for heating ham
    2 tablespoons butter
    ¼ pound chopped fresh mushrooms
    1 small green pepper, seeded and chopped
    2 tablespoons flour
    1½ cups milk
    salt and pepper to taste
    1 egg yolk
    6 hard-cooked eggs, sliced
    1 teaspoon lemon juice

Heat ham slices in skillet with butter or bacon fat. Melt butter in saucepan, add mushrooms and green pepper. Cook until vegetables are limp. Stir in flour. Add milk, blend, and cook, stirring, until sauce begins to thicken. Season with salt and pepper, stir in egg yolk. Add egg slices. Cook over very low heat only until thoroughly hot. Remove from stove, stir in lemon juice. Spoon onto heated ham slices and serve.

CHICKEN LIVERS AND SCRAMBLED EGGS IN PATTY SHELLS
SERVES FOUR

    4 patty shells (frozen or from the bakery)
    2 chicken livers
    1 tablespoon butter
    1 tablespoon chopped green pepper
    1 teaspoon Worcestershire sauce
    salt and pepper to taste
    6 eggs
    butter for scrambling

Place patty shells in oven to heat. Sauté chicken livers in butter until no longer pink. Chop coarsely in pan. Add green pepper. Cook, stirring, until limp. Blend in Worcestershire sauce. Add salt and pepper to taste. Remove from heat, cover, set aside while you scramble eggs as per basic instructions. Combine chicken livers and scrambled egg. Pile into heated patty shells and serve. Good with broiled peaches.

OEUFS AU BEURRE NOIR
SERVES FOUR

    8 eggs
    2 tablespoons butter
    1 tablespoon lemon juice
    salt and coarse-ground black pepper to taste

Butter 4 individual ramekins; break 2 eggs into each. Place in preheated 350°F. oven. Melt butter in saucepan. Just before egg whites have set, turn heat high under butter and stir in lemon juice. When sizzling and a deep nutlike brown, remove ramekins from oven and pour butter over eggs. The heat of the butter will complete the cooking. Season with salt and pepper and serve in ramekins, along with crisp bacon, beaten biscuits and comb honey.

OEUFS À LA FLORENTINE
SERVES FOUR

    1 10-ounce package frozen leaf spinach
    2 tablespoons butter
    salt and pepper to taste
    onion salt to taste
    4 tablespoons heavy cream
    2 tablespoons grated Parmesan cheese
    8 eggs

Thaw frozen spinach overnight in refrigerator. Add to heated butter in saucepan. Cook, stirring frequently, only until thoroughly heated. (Alternate method: Cook frozen spinach according to package directions; drain well, pressing out all water; combine with soft, room-temperature butter.) Season with salt and pepper and onion salt. Place in the bottom of well-buttered baking dish or 4 individual ramekins. Blend cream with cheese and pour half of mixture over spinach. Break eggs over cream, spoon remaining cream and cheese over eggs. Bake at 350°F. until egg whites have set. Serve with broiled Canadian bacon.

SCRAMBLED EGGS WITH OYSTERS À LA LOUISIANE
SERVES TWO TO FOUR

4 to 6 large fresh oysters and their liquid
3 tablespoons butter
1 clove garlic (optional)
1 tablespoon minced onion
1 tablespoon green pepper, seeded and minced
4 eggs
1 tablespoon cream
1 tablespoon liquid used in cooking oysters
chopped parsley

Simmer oysters in liquid until edges curl (2 to 3 minutes); drain, reserving 1 tablespoon of the liquid. Chop oysters coarsely, set aside. Melt butter in saucepan, add garlic, onion, and green pepper. Cook over medium heat until vegetables are limp. Remove and discard garlic. Beat eggs lightly with cream and oyster liquid. Pour over vegetables, stir once to blend, add oysters. Cook, stirring, until almost done to your taste. Heat of pan will continue cooking. Transfer to serving platter. Garnish with chopped parsley and serve.

SPLENDIFEROUS EGGS
SERVES FOUR

    4 eggs
    2 tablespoons butter
    ½ cup heavy cream
    ½ teaspoon salt
    ¼ teaspoon pepper

Break eggs into bowl, beat slightly—only until yolks and whites are well mixed. Scramble in 1 tablespoon butter in top half of double boiler over simmering water. When eggs begin to set, stir in the cream and remaining butter. Season with salt and pepper. Don't overcook; they should be creamy and quite soft. Serve with thin slices of smoked salmon.

FRIED EGGS PIPÉRADE
SERVES SIX

    1 large green pepper, seeded and cut into thin
        strips
    1 medium-sized Bermuda onion, chopped
    1 small clove garlic
    2 tablespoons olive oil
    1 No. 2 can (2 cups) Italian-style tomatoes with
        basil
    salt and pepper to taste
    Tabasco sauce
    6 eggs
    butter and olive oil (half and half)

Sauté green pepper, onion, and garlic in oil until limp; remove garlic and discard. Add tomatoes, simmer until quite thick, season with salt, pepper, and Tabasco sauce. Fry eggs in oil and butter as per basic instructions. Place sauce in serving dish and top with fried eggs. Serve with grilled bacon.

OEUFS À LA BOHÉMIENNE
SERVES SIX

6 brioches
2 to 4 truffles, sliced
½ cup dry white wine
2 tablespoons butter
6 eggs, slightly beaten
butter for scrambling
salt to taste

Slice the top from each brioche, scoop out and discard centers. Place in medium oven to heat. Cook truffles, wine, and butter in saucepan until liquid has evaporated. Add to eggs, scramble as per basic instructions. Pile into heated brioches and serve with spicy sausages and fried apple rings.

HUEVOS RANCHEROS
SERVES FOUR

2 slices bacon
2 tablespoons minced onion
1 small can peeled green chiles, chopped
1 No. 2 can (2 cups) solid-pack tomatoes
¼ pound Cheddar cheese, cubed
8 eggs
salt and pepper to taste

Fry bacon in large skillet over low heat. (Do not drain fat from pan.) Remove bacon when crisp, drain on paper towel. Crumble and reserve. Add onion to bacon fat in pan. Cook, stirring, until limp, then add chiles and tomatoes; simmer 5 minutes. Add cheese. When cheese is almost melted, break in eggs, one at a time. Sprinkle with crumbled bacon. Cover pan and cook until egg whites have set. Delicious with hot garlic bread and guava shells.

27

OEUFS SUR LE PLAT LORRAINE
(BAKED EGGS WITH BACON AND CHEESE)
SERVES FOUR

6 strips bacon
½ cup diced Gruyère cheese
8 eggs
¼ cup light cream
salt

Broil or fry bacon until half done; cut into 1-inch pieces. Arrange in the bottom of a buttered, shallow ovenproof dish. Sprinkle cheese over bacon. Break eggs over cheese and pour cream over surface. Sprinkle with salt. Bake in a 325°F. oven for 15 to 20 minutes, or until egg whites have set.

BAKED EGGS IN TOMATO SHELLS
SERVES FOUR

4 large ripe but firm tomatoes
2 teaspoons butter
4 eggs
salt and pepper to taste
2 tablespoons grated Swiss cheese
parsley

Cut a thin slice from the top of each tomato. Scoop out the pulp. Salt lightly and turn upside down to drain for 10 minutes. Arrange in well-buttered baking dish and place ½ teaspoon butter in each. Bake at 350°F. for 5 minutes. Break 1 egg into each shell, bake until egg whites have set. Sprinkle each with salt, pepper, and cheese. Place under broiler until cheese is melted and bubbly. Garnish with parsley and serve with hashed brown potatoes and sausage patties.

Omelets — from France with Love

Omelets, supposedly the acid test of even a great chef, are never difficult to make if you use a proper pan. The pan should be heavy, with sloping sides, and should be well greased at all times. It is wiped clean with a paper towel after each use, and never, but never, is it used for any other purpose. The best omelet pans, in our opinion, are made of iron, a little lighter than cast iron, or of stainless steel. The pans imported from France are preferred, due to the perfect slope of their sides, the length of their handle, and their depth.

Small omelets are easier to handle, so unless and until you are an expert, don't attempt more than 4 eggs at one time. A 7- or 8-inch pan is about the right size for any omelet of 4 eggs or under.

BASIC FRENCH OMELET
SERVES ONE

　　2 eggs
　　salt and pepper to taste
　　1 teaspoon water, milk, or cream (optional)
　　1 teaspoon butter

Beat eggs lightly with fork, season with salt and pepper to taste. Add liquid if desired. Have pan hot before adding butter, and butter sizzling before adding eggs. Pour in the eggs and cook over high heat, stirring once with a fork, as for scrambled eggs. Push the eggs to the center of the pan as they start to congeal. The still-liquid part will then flow into the empty spaces. When firm but still moist, gently tilt pan downward toward you. The omelet will slide down the side of the pan. Fold a third of the omelet over toward the center. Tilt the pan up in the opposite direction and with a spatula roll and fold onto a hot plate. The entire operation takes less time than the telling and the result will be a perfect omelet—oval in shape and a light golden brown.

NOTE: Keep warm in a 200°F. oven while preparing additional omelets.

To Fill Omelets:

Remove from heat before folding and put a few spoonfuls of filling on half of omelet; fold over and roll onto platter or plate.

OMELET AUX FINES HERBES

To each 2 beaten eggs, add 1 to 2 teaspoons of finely chopped mixed herbs: parsley, chives, chervil, tarragon, etc. Cook omelets as per basic instructions. Turn out onto serving plate, pour a little melted butter over surface, and garnish with parsley if desired.

CHEESE OMELET

Beat 2 eggs with 1 teaspoon water, add salt to taste, and blend in 1 tablespoon grated cheese. Cook omelet in the usual way.

INDIAN OMELET

Heat 1 cup bottled chutney (chop up large pieces). Make 2 2-egg omelets, adding a pinch of curry powder to each before cooking. Fill with a little of the hot chutney. Spoon remainder over omelets on serving plate.

HAM AND OLIVE OMELET

Sauté 1 small peeled, seeded, and chopped tomato in 1 tablespoon butter; add ¼ cup diced cooked ham. Beat 4 eggs lightly, add 2 tablespoons thin-sliced pimiento-stuffed green olives. Make 2 small or 1 large omelet; fill with some of the ham and tomato mixture. Spoon remainder over and around cooked omelet.

CHICKEN LIVER AND PARSLEY OMELET

Sauté 2 chicken livers in butter until no longer pink. Chop or slice into small pieces. Add 1 large chopped fresh mushroom. Cook until mushroom is tender. Beat 4 eggs slightly, add 1 tablespoon minced parsley. Make 2 small or 1 large omelet. Fill with chicken livers and mushrooms before folding.

CROÛTON OMELET WITH ONIONS AND CHEESE

Cook 1 tablespoon minced onion in 1 tablespoon butter until soft. Add ¼ cup garlic-seasoned croûtons. Stir until they have soaked up all the butter. Beat 4 eggs lightly, add 1 tablespoon grated cheese, the onions, and the croûton mixture. Make 1 large or 2 small omelets; cook in the usual way.

CHORIZO AND PEPPER OMELET

Sauté 2 tablespoons chopped green pepper with ¼ cup chopped chorizo (Spanish spicy sausage) until peppers are limp. Make 2 2-egg omelets; fill each with some of the mixture, spoon remainder around cooked omelets.

STRAWBERRY AND SOUR CREAM OMELET

Slice thinly ½ cup fresh strawberries; sprinkle with 1 teaspoon confectioners' sugar. Make 1 large or 2 small omelets in the usual way. Before folding, spread with sour cream, then spoon strawberries over the cream. Fold, and sprinkle surface with sugar. Run under hot broiler a few moments. Garnish with additional sliced strawberries.

BLUEBERRY OMELET

Make in the same way as strawberry omelet, substituting whole fresh blueberries. (Fresh cream may be used instead of sour cream, and completely thawed frozen fruit used if fresh fruit is not available.)

OMELET À LA FLORENTINE

Cook omelet in the usual manner; fill with creamed spinach purée.

CAVIAR OMELET

Make a 2-egg omelet for each serving. Fill with a little caviar and serve with sour cream.

MUSHROOM OMELET

Sauté ½ pound of mushrooms, chopped fine, in 2 table-spoons of butter until they are pale golden brown. Add 1 tablespoon dry sherry; cover the pan and simmer gently for 1 to 2 minutes. Blend in 2 tablespoons of heavy cream. Make 2 2-egg omelets; fill with some of the cooked mushrooms. (Remove from pan with slotted spoon.) Pour remaining mushrooms and sauce over each omelet just before serving.

CHIPPED BEEF OMELET

Sauté ½ cup of chipped beef in 1 tablespoon of butter. Stir in 1 tablespoon of heavy cream. Make 2 2-egg omelets; fill with chipped beef mixture.

SHRIMP OMELET

Cook 1 dozen raw, shelled, and deveined shrimp in enough dry white wine to cover for 10 minutes. Drain, reserve 4 whole shrimp. Chop remainder. Melt 2 tablespoons butter in heavy saucepan. Add 1 teaspoon minced onion and stir over medium heat until onion is transparent. Add the chopped shrimp, a generous tablespoon of prepared tomato sauce, and 1 teaspoon grated Parmesan cheese. Season with salt and a dash of Tabasco sauce. Fill 2 2-egg omelets. Garnish with the whole shrimp and serve with tomato sauce.

JELLY OMELET

Make omelets in the usual manner. Fill before folding with tart jelly; before turning from pan, sprinkle lightly with sugar and run under hot broiler for 10 seconds. Serve at once.

CORN AND CHEESE OMELET

Add 1 teaspoon grated Gruyère cheese, a pinch of salt, and
¼ cup whole kernel corn (cooked, fresh, or canned) to each
2 slightly beaten eggs. Blend and make omelets in the usual
way.

*We could keep adding variation after variation to the versatile omelet since, as I'm sure you know, it can be filled with
almost anything—from truffles and imported pâté to the remains of last night's roast. Though a glamorous dish indeed,
it is one that is thrifty too. So on to the kitchen. Just to prove
our point, here are recipes that make use of those tasty bits,
pieces, and half-cups of leftover food which might otherwise
be left to dry up on the back shelf of the refrigerator. Each
of the following omelets is made in just a little different way
to add excitement to your cooking and interest to your meal.*

OMELET PARMENTIER
SERVES FOUR

> 2 tablespoons olive oil
> 2 tablespoons butter
> 1 cup diced, leftover boiled potatoes
> 1 tablespoon chopped chives
> ½ teaspoon salt
> 5 large or 6 small eggs, well beaten

Heat the oil and butter in a large omelet pan, add potatoes
and chives, and cook over medium flame for 2 to 3 minutes,
chopping potatoes fine as they cook. Season with salt. Pour
in the eggs (lift potatoes so that moist eggs can run under
them). When mixture is firm but still moist, transfer pan to
preheated oven broiler. Cook about 4 inches from flame until
surface is firm and lightly browned. Turn out onto a pre-

heated round serving plate. Cut omelet into pie-shaped wedges. Serve with broiled Canadian bacon.

PUFFY VIRGINIA HAM OMELET
SERVES TWO

  4 eggs, separated
  3 teaspoons warm water
  ¼ to ½ cup baked leftover ham, finely minced
  salt to taste
  2 tablespoons butter

Beat egg whites until stiff. Add warm water to yolks, beat until light and lemony, blend in ham and salt to taste (amount depends on saltiness of ham), and fold in beaten egg whites. Melt the butter in an 8- to 9-inch omelet pan. Pour in the egg mixture. Cook over medium flame, without stirring, until bottom sets. Transfer to a preheated 350°F. oven and bake until top is a light golden brown. Serve at once.

OMELET CLAMART
SERVES TWO

  2 tablespoons butter
  2 tablespoons flour
  ½ teaspoon salt
  1 cup milk
  1 cup cooked leftover miniature green peas
  ¼ cup chopped pimientos
  4 eggs
  2 teaspoons water
  ½ teaspoon salt
  2 tablespoons grated Swiss cheese
  1 tablespoon butter

Melt the butter in a heavy saucepan; add the flour and salt. Stir over medium flame until bubbly. Slowly add the milk. Cook, stirring frequently, until sauce thickens. Blend in the peas and pimientos. Cover surface of sauce with waxed paper to keep film from forming, set aside while making omelets. Beat eggs with water, add salt and cheese, and blend well. Heat butter in omelet pan until sizzling. Pour in eggs. Cook until eggs are set but still soft (see basic omelet instructions). Remove from flame. Spoon half the creamed peas into the center, fold, and turn out onto serving platter. Surround with remaining creamed peas and hot buttered toast points. Serve with little link sausages.

OMELET AUX CROÛTONS
SERVES TWO

2 slices leftover white bread
1 tablespoon butter
1 tablespoon tomato paste
1 or 2 dashes Tabasco sauce
¼ teaspoon pepper
¼ teaspoon salt
¼ teaspoon garlic salt
4 eggs
1 tablespoon water
¼ teaspoon salt
2 tablespoons grated Parmesan cheese

Remove crust from bread. Cut into small squares. Sauté in the butter until limp. Add the tomato paste, Tabasco sauce, pepper, salt, and garlic salt. Remove from the fire, mash with a fork until smooth. Set aside while you make omelet. Combine eggs with water, salt, and cheese. Melt butter in omelet pan; when sizzling pour in eggs. Cook in the usual way (see basic omelet instructions). When firm, spread with bread mixture. Fold and roll omelet out onto serving plate. Serve with sausage patties.

36

OMELET AU FROMAGE
GRAND-MÈRE
SERVES FOUR

    1 cup soft bread crumbs
    1 cup milk
    6 eggs
    salt and pepper to taste
    2 tablespoons grated sharp cheese
    2 tablespoons melted butter

Cover bread crumbs with milk, let stand 5 minutes. Beat eggs until light, season with salt and pepper. Combine with milk and bread crumb mixture. Pour into well-buttered, shallow ovenproof dish. Bake at 325°F. until firm (20 to 25 minutes). Mix grated cheese with melted butter and sprinkle over surface. Place under broiler until lightly browned. Serve with tart jelly.

The Secret of
Soufflés

Soufflés are for a wedding breakfast or a party brunch—for Sunday's late meal and for New Year's Day. But they are also for any time you want to serve someone special—it could be your own special family—something especially good.

A soufflé, despite its elegance and glamour, is surprisingly easy to make. It is nothing more than a white sauce or cream sauce with flavoring plus cheese or a purée of other ingredients into which stiffly beaten egg whites have been carefully folded. As with the perfect omelet, the secret of a successful soufflé lies not in "what's in it" but in how it is made.

To begin, when a sufficient quantity of air is beaten into the egg whites, the soufflé will rise as it cooks, to a magnificent puff. To achieve this very necessary volume of air, you must put aside your electric or rotary beater and beat the egg whites by hand. Now don't despair and give up before you start. You can do this job quickly and with ease if you use that small and very efficient little implement the French call a fouet, which is simply an oval-shaped wire whisk or whip. In addition, you must, of course, have a mixing bowl and a saucepan for making the sauce. But the most important item is a straight-sided porcelain mold. Although a soufflé may be baked in just about anything (scooped-out tomatoes

and green pepper shells are fun for a change), it will rise to its peak of perfection only in this French-inspired dish.

You will find the whisk and the mold in any number of sizes in the housewares department of most large stores, as well as in small gourmet shops that carry French cooking equipment.

Anything else? Only the "know-how" to be sure, and here it is—a basic soufflé recipe—plus additions and adaptations. One, two, three, step by easy step.

BASIC SOUFFLÉ
SERVES FOUR

PREPARE BAKING DISH: Generously butter a 1½- or 2-quart soufflé mold; place 2 or 3 tablespoons of fine dry bread crumbs, grated cheese, flour, or sugar (depending on the type of soufflé) in the bottom. Rotate mold to distribute this coating evenly—then turn it upsidedown and give it a good tap to get rid of any surplus. Place in refrigerator to chill while you prepare soufflé.

MAKE SAUCE: Melt 3 tablespoons butter in a heavy saucepan. Stir in 3 tablespoons flour, and blend until bubbly. Slowly pour in 1 cup of milk. Stir over medium flame with wire whisk until sauce begins to thicken. Remove from heat. Fold into basic sauce from ¾ to 1 cup grated or crumbled cheese; minced or puréed vegetables; purée of fruit; or cooked finely diced or minced fish, seafood, fowl, or meat—plus appropriate seasoning.* Add 4 egg yolks, one at a time, beating well after each addition.

BEAT EGG WHITES: Place 5 egg whites in large mixing bowl. Add a pinch of salt and beat by hand with a wire whisk

---

* Sauce may be made ahead up to this point. Dot surface with tiny slivers of butter and cover closely with waxed paper to keep film from forming. Refrigerate if not used in 30 minutes.

39

until 7 or 8 times their original volume. They should be still moist but firm, and stiff enough to stand in peaks when beater is removed.

FOLD INTO SAUCE: Use the same wire whisk to blend about ¼ of the beaten whites into the basic sauce. Then gently fold in the remaining whites with rubber or wooden spatula, cutting them in quickly by lifting the mixture from the bottom of the saucepan and folding over and over. The entire process should take less than a minute. Don't overblend; it is far better to have a few white patches in a light and airy soufflé than one that will not rise.

BAKE: As soon as batter is blended, pour it into prepared soufflé dish. Place on center rack of preheated 400°F. oven. Immediately reduce heat to 375°F., bake for 25 to 30 minutes or until soufflé is puffed and light golden brown.

CHEESE SOUFFLÉ I

Coat soufflé dish with grated Parmesan cheese. Proceed as in basic soufflé recipe, adding ¾ cup grated Swiss cheese, ½ teaspoon salt, and a dash of cayenne pepper to sauce.

CHEESE SOUFFLÉ II

Coat soufflé dish with fine dry bread crumbs. Proceed as in basic soufflé recipe, adding ¾ cup crumbled Cheddar cheese to sauce. Season with a dash of Tabasco sauce and ½ teaspoon salt.

ONION SOUFFLÉ

Peel and chop 4 medium Italian (purple) onions. Place in water to cover, boil until very soft, and drain well (reserving

¼ cup of the water). Chop fine and drain again. Set aside. Proceed as in basic soufflé recipe, substituting ¾ cup light cream and ¼ cup onion water for the milk. Add the chopped onions to basic sauce, season with ¼ teaspoon salt.

SHRIMP SOUFFLÉ

Melt 1 tablespoon butter in saucepan, add 1 tablespoon chopped onion; cook, stirring, over medium flame until onion is limp. Add ½ pound peeled and deveined, coarsely chopped raw shrimp and ¼ cup dry white wine. Cover and cook for 10 minutes. Uncover and cook until all liquid has evaporated. Remove from pan and chop very fine. Set aside. Coat buttered soufflé mold with fine dry bread crumbs. Proceed as in basic soufflé, adding shrimp to sauce.

MUSHROOM SOUFFLÉ

Clean and chop very fine ½ pound fresh mushrooms. Melt 1 tablespoon butter in a saucepan. Add 1 tablespoon chopped onion and cook, stirring, until onion is limp but not brown. Add the mushrooms and 1 tablespoon dry sherry. Cook over medium heat, stirring frequently, until all moisture has evaporated. Set aside. Coat soufflé mold with grated Parmesan cheese and proceed as in basic soufflé. Add mushroom mixture to basic sauce. Season with ½ teaspoon salt.

BROCCOLI SOUFFLÉ

Cook a 10-ounce package of frozen broccoli in salted water until barely tender. Drain thoroughly, discard any tough stalks, and chop coarsely. Place on bottom of buttered soufflé mold. Proceed as in basic soufflé, adding ¾ cup grated Swiss cheese to sauce. Pour soufflé batter over broccoli, place soufflé mold in pan of hot water, and bake at 350°F. for 35 to 40 minutes or until soufflé is well puffed and light golden brown.

CHICKEN SOUFFLÉ AMANDINE

Blend ¾ cup finely minced cooked white meat of chicken with ¼ cup blanched toasted and finely slivered almonds. Coat soufflé dish with flour. Proceed as in basic soufflé, adding chicken-almond mixture to sauce. Season with ½ teaspoon salt and ¼ teaspoon pepper.

SPINACH-CHEESE SOUFFLÉ

Wash and cook 2 pounds fresh spinach, drain well, chop very fine, and purée in a blender or force through a coarse sieve. Place in saucepan with 1 tablespoon butter, and season with ½ teaspoon salt, ¼ teaspoon pepper, and a dash of nutmeg. Cook over low heat, stirring constantly, until all liquid has evaporated. Stir in 1 tablespoon grated Swiss cheese and set aside. Coat soufflé mold with fine dry bread crumbs. Proceed as in basic soufflé. Add prepared spinach-cheese mixture to sauce.

DEVILED HAM AND APPLESAUCE SOUFFLÉ

Cover the bottom of a well-buttered soufflé mold with a thin layer of smooth applesauce. Proceed as directed for basic soufflé, blending 1 small can of Smithfield ham spread into sauce. Pour soufflé batter over applesauce in mold. Place mold in a pan of hot water and bake at 375°F. until soufflé has set.

Must a soufflé be served the minute it's cooked? Most cookbooks say yes, it absolutely must—and they're right, of course, but we do feel they are just a bit overcautious. Certainly, it's best to wait for the soufflé rather than have the soufflé wait for you. However, if properly blended and baked, it can remain in the oven from 3 to 5 minutes longer than planned and when brought to the table it will "hold up," retaining its elegant shape for the time needed to assemble and seat your guests.

For a large party or a buffet it's better to make small soufflés in individual molds. They will remain puffy much longer than one large one. If made in ring molds or in vegetable shells, they will not rise to an awe-inspiring height, but they will "stand" for some time and look grand as can be on a buffet sideboard or table.

Here are a few ideas for soufflés at high noon.

PETITS SOUFFLÉS AU FROMAGE
SERVES SIX

    1 teaspoon minced onion
    1 cup milk
    2 dashes Tabasco sauce
    2½ cups soft bread crumbs
    ½ cup grated Parmesan cheese
    1 tablespoon butter
    6 eggs, separated

Butter and chill 6 individual soufflé dishes. Combine the minced onion and milk, then bring to a boil in large saucepan. Remove from heat and add Tabasco sauce, bread crumbs, cheese, and butter. Blend, then beat in the egg yolks. Beat egg whites until stiff, fold into first mixture. Fill soufflé dishes ¾ full. Place them in a pan of hot water. Bake at 375°F. for 15 minutes or until well puffed and a light golden brown. Serve with grilled tomato slices and crisp bacon.

EASY SHRIMP AND CHEESE SOUFFLÉ
SERVES SIX

      fine dry bread crumbs
      1 can (10 ounces) frozen condensed cream of
         shrimp soup, thawed
      1 cup shredded sharp Cheddar cheese
      6 egg yolks
      ½ cup minced cooked shrimp
      1 tablespoon dry sherry
      6 egg whites.

Butter generously a 2-quart soufflé dish. Sprinkle bottom and sides with bread crumbs. Place in refrigerator to chill. Combine soup and cheese, cook over very low flame until cheese melts. Remove from heat. Add egg yolks, one at a time, beating after each addition. Blend in shrimp and sherry. Beat egg whites until stiff, gently fold into soup mixture. Pour into prepared mold and bake at 375°F. for 35 to 40 minutes, or until just firm to the touch. Serve with broiled apricot halves.

HAM SOUFFLÉ IN GREEN PEPPERS
SERVES FOUR

      8 large green peppers
      3 tablespoons butter
      3 tablespoons flour
      ¾ cup milk
      1 4½-ounce can deviled ham
      3 eggs, separated

Cut a thin slice from the stem end of each green pepper. Scoop out all seeds and pulp. Parboil in salted water for 10 minutes. Drain well, set aside. Melt butter in heavy sauce-pan, stir in flour, and cook until bubbly. Slowly add milk and cook, stirring, until sauce thickens; remove from heat. Add deviled ham. Blend and beat in egg yolks. Beat whites until stiff. Fold into deviled ham mixture. Spoon into the green peppers. Place in shallow buttered baking pan. Bake at 375°F. for 15 to 20 minutes or until soufflés have set. Serve with pickled peaches.

VEGETABLE SOUFFLÉ RING WITH CHIPPED BEEF IN SHERRIED CREAM SAUCE
SERVES SIX

VEGETABLE SOUFFLÉ RING

1½ cups cooked green peas
1½ cups cooked diced carrots
¼ cup chopped green onion
¼ cup beef broth or stock
4 egg yolks
½ cup cream
⅔ cup fine dry bread crumbs
salt and pepper to taste
5 egg whites

Place peas, carrots, onion, and beef broth in electric blender and purée. Pour into mixing bowl. Stir in egg yolks, cream, and bread crumbs. Season to taste with salt and pepper. Beat egg whites until stiff. Fold into vegetable mixture. Pour into buttered ring mold and bake in preheated 400°F. oven for 30 minutes or until firm to the touch. Let stand for a minute, then turn out onto round serving plate. Fill center with creamed chipped beef.

CREAMED CHIPPED BEEF

2 tablespoons butter
2 tablespoons flour
1½ cups milk
3 tablespoons dry sherry
2 2½-ounce jars dried chipped beef
1 egg yolk
parsley

Melt butter in saucepan. Stir in flour, cook until bubbly, slowly add milk. Cook, stirring, over low heat until sauce begins to thicken; add sherry and beef. Cook until thoroughly heated. Stir in egg yolk. Cook, stirring constantly, 1 minute more. Pour into center of vegetable soufflé ring. Garnish with parsley and serve.

SHRIMP SOUFFLÉ NEW ORLEANS
SERVES SIX

SHRIMP SAUCE

5 tablespoons butter
2 pounds cooked shrimp, peeled and deveined
¼ cup cognac
2 tablespoons diced green pepper
2 tablespoons chopped onion
1 crushed clove garlic (optional)
4 fresh tomatoes, peeled, seeded, and chopped
1 cup tomato sauce
2 or 3 dashes Tabasco sauce
½ teaspoon salt
½ teaspoon coarse-ground black pepper
1 bay leaf

Melt 2 tablespoons butter in a heavy skillet over medium flame, add shrimp, and stir until thoroughly heated. Pour in the cognac, ignite, and shake pan until flame dies out. Remove from heat, set aside. In separate saucepan, sauté green pepper, onion, and garlic in the remaining butter until limp but not brown; add remaining ingredients and simmer gently for 15 to 20 minutes. Remove bay leaf; combine with shrimp and any liquid from skillet. Set aside to cool while you prepare soufflé (or refrigerate until ready to use).

SOUFFLÉ

> 2 tablespoons butter
> 2 tablespoons flour
> 1 cup milk
> ¼ teaspoon salt
> 1 teaspoon grated Parmesan cheese
> 3 egg yolks
> 5 egg whites

Butter and flour 2-quart soufflé mold. Place in refrigerator to chill. Melt butter in saucepan, stir until bubbly. Slowly add milk and cook, stirring, until sauce thickens. Remove from heat; blend in salt and cheese. Add egg yolks one at a time, beating after each addition. Beat whites until stiff, fold into first mixture (see basic soufflé instructions). Place half of the cooked shrimp sauce into prepared mold, pour soufflé mixture over sauce. Place in pan of hot water and bake at 375°F. for 25 to 30 minutes or until soufflé is well puffed and a golden brown. Reheat remaining sauce. Pass at the table to spoon over each portion of the soufflé.

Griddle Cakes, Pancakes, and Crêpes

"Pancakes and fritters say the bells of St. Peter's," and very proper that they do. Nothing could be better for a Sunday morning meal. Add spicy sausage or crisp bacon and invite the bishop or the boss and his wife, or simply serve them to that favorite man in your life, a few friends, and you.

To start, there are plain griddle cakes—though that adjective seems unfair. They certainly don't taste plain when served hot from the griddle, with maple syrup or honey, and butter.

Make the batter ahead if you like, or mix it up quickly in the morning. Either way, with a "decent-sized" griddle, they take almost no time at all, or at least no more time than they are worth in your family's appreciation.

PLAIN GRIDDLE CAKES
SERVES FOUR TO SIX

2 cups flour
1½ teaspoons baking powder
1 teaspoon salt
2 eggs
1½ cups milk
¼ teaspoon vanilla
2 tablespoons melted butter

Sift dry ingredients into mixing bowl. Stir in eggs, milk, vanilla, and butter. Blend well. If possible, let batter stand 30 minutes or more. Heat griddle. Pour on batter in uniform amounts from pitcher or tip of large spoon. Cook cakes over medium heat until bubbly on top. Turn and brown underside. Serve at once or keep warm in oven while making additional cakes.

BLUEBERRY GRIDDLE CAKES

Add ¾ cup canned, frozen (thawed) or fresh blueberries to batter.

RASPBERRY GRIDDLE CAKES

Add ¾ cup fresh raspberries to batter.

STRAWBERRY GRIDDLE CAKES

Add ¾ cup fresh, chopped, well-drained strawberries to batter.

DRIED BEEF GRIDDLE CAKES

Add ½ cup finely shredded dried beef to batter.

APPLE GRIDDLE CAKES

Peel, core, and chop fine 1 medium-sized apple. Stir into batter just before cooking cakes.

COTTAGE CHEESE
GRIDDLE CAKES
SERVES FOUR TO SIX

1 cup creamy cottage cheese
½ cup cream
2 eggs
2 tablespoons sugar
4 tablespoons flour
½ teaspoon salt
½ teaspoon baking powder
¼ teaspoon vanilla

Mash cottage cheese smooth with fork. Add cream and eggs, and blend until smooth (or place cottage cheese, cream, and eggs in electric blender, and blend until smooth). Add remaining ingredients, blend with wire whisk. Grease skillet with butter. Cook cakes until lightly browned, turning once.

CORNMEAL GRIDDLE CAKES
VIEUX CARRÉ
SERVES SIX TO EIGHT

2 cups flour
1 teaspoon salt
2 teaspoons baking powder
½ cup cornmeal
¼ teaspoon vanilla
1½ cups milk
2 eggs, lightly beaten
2 tablespoons melted butter (cooled)

Sift flour with salt and baking powder. Add cornmeal. Add vanilla to milk, blend with eggs and melted butter. Mix into dry ingredients. Blend well. Bake on a hot, lightly greased griddle.

BUTTERMILK GRIDDLE CAKES
SERVES FOUR TO SIX

1⅓ cups flour
⅛ teaspoon salt
½ teaspoon soda
2 cups buttermilk
2 tablespoons melted butter
1 tablespoon sugar

Sift flour, salt, and soda into mixing bowl. Stir in buttermilk, blend until smooth. Blend in butter and sugar. Drop by spoonfuls onto lightly greased griddle. Cook until brown on both sides, turning once. Nice with spicy sausage, molasses, or corn syrup.

After griddle cakes come pancakes, or maybe before. As every good cook knows, they are really interchangeable, give or take a teaspoon of flour.

Just for the record, and in case you're confused, griddle-cake batter should be thick enough to hold its shape and form perfect round cakes when poured out, while pancake batter is thinner and takes on the shape of the pan.

BASIC PANCAKES
SERVES FOUR

1 cup flour
½ teaspoon salt
1¼ cups milk
3 eggs

Sift flour and salt, add milk and eggs, then beat until smooth. Heat small skillet, grease lightly, and pour in enough batter

51

to just cover bottom of pan. Tilt pan so batter is evenly distributed. Cook until brown on underside, bubbly on top. Turn and brown second side. Repeat until all batter has been used. Serve with butter and syrup or spread with jam or jelly; roll up and serve dusted with confectioners' sugar.

DEVILED HAM PANCAKES

Spread cooked cakes with deviled ham spread. Roll up and serve with strawberry jam.

APPLESAUCE PANCAKES DELUXE

Spread cooked cakes with applesauce. Roll up. Place, just touching, in buttered, shallow baking dish. Cover surface completely with sour cream. Sprinkle with brown sugar. Place directly under broiler flame until bubbly and lightly browned.

PANCAKE CAKE

Make large pancakes from basic batter recipe, using a 7- to 8-inch pan. Spread each cake as it's cooked with soft butter and tart jelly. Stack cooked cakes, layer-cake fashion. Cut and serve in wedges at the table.

PANCAKES WITH POACHED EGGS AND BACON

Make large (7- to 8-inch) cakes from basic pancake recipe. For each serving, top one cake with bacon strips. Cover with second cake. Top with poached egg. Serve with comb honey.

GRAHAM CRACKER CRUMB PANCAKES
SERVES SIX

2½ cups flour
½ cup (commercial) graham cracker crumbs
1 tablespoon baking powder
1 teaspoon salt
¼ cup sugar
2 cups milk
2 tablespoons melted butter
3 eggs, lightly beaten

Mix dry ingredients. Add milk and melted butter to eggs. Combine the mixtures. Blend well. Melt a little butter in a small frying pan. Add 1 tablespoon batter and rotate pan to spread evenly over entire surface. Brown on both sides, turning once. Keep cakes warm in very low oven until all batter has been used.

POTATO PANCAKES
SERVES SIX

6 medium-sized potatoes
2 tablespoons flour
1 egg
1 tablespoon minced onion
1½ teaspoons salt
1 tablespoon melted butter
vegetable oil

Peel and grate the potatoes medium fine. Plunge immediately into cold water. Let stand 10 minutes. Place in four thicknesses of cheesecloth. Squeeze out as much water as possible.

Place in mixing bowl and add remaining ingredients, except oil, in order listed.

Heat a small amount of oil in heavy skillet. Use 2 tablespoons mixture for each pancake. Use back of spoon to flatten out in pan. Fry until crisp, turning once. Drain on paper towel (add additional oil as needed). Serve hot with chilled applesauce.

BANANA PANCAKE BAKE
SERVES TWO

> 3 to 4 ripe but firm bananas
> 8 tablespoons melted butter
> 6 tablespoons sugar
> ½ teaspoon grated lemon rind
> ¼ teaspoon cinnamon
> ⅛ teaspoon nutmeg
> 2 eggs, beaten
> ½ cup milk
> ½ cup flour
> ¼ teaspoon salt

Slice bananas into heavy skillet; add 3 tablespoons butter. Sauté over low flame until bananas are slightly soft. Add 2 tablespoons sugar, the lemon rind, cinnamon, and nutmeg. Cook, stirring, until sugar has dissolved. Set aside but keep warm or reheat.

Combine eggs with milk, stir in flour and salt. Beat with wire whisk until smooth. Heat 1 tablespoon butter in second ovenproof skillet. Pour in batter, place in preheated 450°F. oven. Bake until it puffs up (approximately 5 minutes), prick with fork; bake 10 minutes at same heat, pricking several times, then reduce heat and cook a final 10 minutes. Remove from oven, sprinkle surface with 2 tablespoons butter and 2 tablespoons sugar. Spoon banana mixture over half the

surface, fold over like an omelet and turn out onto platter.
Sprinkle with remaining sugar and butter and serve.

*Crêpes for breakfast? Oh yes indeed! Light as air, crisp and
delicious, they're marvelous spread with butter and jam, or
simply dusted with sugar and served plain. Add juice or fruit
and café au lait and you will be eating the favorite breakfast
of Empress Josephine. Filled with creamed chicken or seafood, crêpes add elegance to a late breakfast buffet.*

*They are time-consuming to make, we have to admit, but—
isn't it wonderful—they can be made ahead, frozen, and then
reheated. Simply cool, then place in stacks of a dozen, with
a double layer of waxed paper between each crêpe. Wrap
in foil and store away in your freezer. Reheat, frozen, in a
medium oven. A few minutes is all it takes.*

BASIC CRÊPES
MAKES TWENTY-FOUR TO THIRTY CRÊPES

3 eggs
pinch of salt
1 teaspoon sugar
1 cup milk
½ teaspoon vanilla
1 cup flour
2 tablespoons melted butter (cooled)

Beat eggs until light and "lemony." Blend in salt, sugar, milk,
and vanilla. Add flour and beat with a wire whisk until batter
is smooth. Blend in melted butter. Let batter "stand" 1 or 2
hours before making crêpes.

Grease 5- or 6-inch crêpe pan generously with soft butter.
Heat to sizzling. Pour in a generous tablespoon of batter;
quickly rotate and tilt pan so that batter completely covers

bottom in a thin layer. Cook over medium heat until brown on bottom, turn to brown other side. Turn out and repeat until all batter has been used. Keep crêpes warm in a very low oven, covered with an inverted bowl, until ready to serve. Serve dusted with confectioners' sugar, or with honey, jam, or syrup.

CRÊPES LOUISE
SERVES SIX

> 2 tablespoons butter
> 2 tablespoons flour
> 1½ cups milk
> ½ teaspoon salt
> ¼ teaspoon white pepper
> 2 tablespoons dry sherry
> 1 egg yolk
> ½ pound flaked crab meat (canned, frozen, or fresh)
> 3 tablespoons heavy cream, whipped stiff
> 24 to 30 small cooked crêpes (see basic crêpes recipe)

Melt butter in saucepan. Stir in flour. When bubbly, slowly add milk, stirring constantly. Cook over low heat, stirring frequently, until sauce thickens. Remove from heat and season with salt and pepper. Add sherry, blend, and stir in egg yolk. Pour off and reserve half the sauce. Add crab meat to remaining sauce in pan. Return to heat and cook, stirring, until quite thick. (Do not allow to boil.) Spread cooked crêpes with this mixture. Roll up and place in single layer in shallow buttered baking dish. Blend whipped cream into reserved sauce. Spread evenly over rolled crêpes, covering them completely. Place in preheated 350°F. oven for 5 minutes, then place directly under broiler flame until surface blisters. Serve very hot.

NOTE: Both crêpes and sauce may be made ahead, then assembled and baked at the last minute.

CRÊPES HÉLÈNE
SERVES SIX

24 to 30 small cooked crêpes (see basic crêpe
  recipe)
¾ cup bitter Seville marmalade
¼ cup blanched slivered almonds
2 tablespoons confectioners' sugar
¾ cup sour cream
1 tablespoon grated orange rind

Spread cooked crêpes with marmalade. Roll up and place in
single layer in shallow greased baking dish. Fold almonds
and sugar into sour cream. Spread over surface of crêpes.
Sprinkle with orange rind. Bake in preheated 350°F. oven
for 5 minutes. Then place directly under high broiler flame
until surface is blistered. Serve at once.

CRÊPES RICOTTA
SERVES SIX

½ pound ricotta cheese
¼ cup sugar
2 tablespoons finely diced candied fruit
2 tablespoons ground almonds
1 egg, well beaten
24 small cooked crêpes (see basic crêpe recipe)
confectioners' sugar

Cream ricotta cheese with sugar until smooth; mix in remaining ingredients. Spoon a little of this mixture on each crêpe.
Roll up. Place, not touching, in single layer on flat tray.
Freeze until firm. Wrap in foil and store in freezer until
ready to bake. Place frozen on baking sheet. Bake at 350°F.
for about 20 minutes, or until thoroughly heated. Dust with
confectioners' sugar and serve warm.

NOTE: Although these crêpes may, of course, be baked without freezing, for some reason they taste lighter and fluffier after a few hours in the cold. They are breakfast fare deluxe and wonderful to have on hand for unexpected guests.

BAKED CRÊPES NEW ORLEANS
SERVES FOUR

　　1 cup confectioners' sugar
　　1 teaspoon anise liqueur
　　1 egg yolk
　　2 dozen cooked crêpes (see basic crêpe recipe)
　　2 tablespoons melted butter
　　confectioners' sugar

Mash the anise liqueur into the confectioners' sugar. Add the egg yolk and beat with a wire whisk to a smooth paste. Place a generous teaspoon of this mixture just off the center of each cooked crêpe. Fold one side of crêpe over the filling, fold ends in, and roll up. Place in a single layer on a buttered baking sheet, brush with melted butter. Bake at 375°F. until browned and well puffed. Dust with confectioners' sugar and serve.

BAKED CRÊPES
WITH CHICKEN HASH
SERVES FOUR TO SIX

　　3 tablespoons butter
　　2 tablespoons flour
　　1 cup milk
　　¼ teaspoon salt
　　1 egg yolk
　　1½ cups diced cooked chicken
　　¼ cup diced sautéed mushrooms

¼ cup slivered blanched almonds
1 teaspoon dry sherry
18 to 20 5-inch cooked crêpes (see basic crêpe recipe)
2 tablespoons Parmesan cheese

Melt 2 tablespoons butter in top half of double boiler, stir in flour, and cook until bubbly; slowly add the milk. Cook, stirring, until sauce thickens slightly. Add salt, stir in egg yolk, and blend quickly with a wire whisk. Place pan over simmering water. Add chicken, mushrooms, almonds, and sherry. Cook, stirring frequently, until quite thick. Remove from heat. Spoon a tablespoon of hash on each crêpe. Roll up, place in shallow ovenproof dish, brush with remainder of the butter, sprinkle with cheese, then bake at 350°F. until cheese has melted and crêpes are thoroughly hot.

Both crêpes and hash may be made ahead, and assembled and baked 15 to 20 minutes before serving.

When you are in the mood for fritters, be in the mood to make them as well. Prepare your batter and fruit ahead if you choose, but fry the fritters at the last minute. These delicate morsels are at their best only when eaten hot from the pan.

BASIC FRITTER BATTER
SERVES SIX TO EIGHT

1⅓ cups flour
¼ teaspoon salt
2 tablespoons sugar
½ cup milk
2 egg yolks, well beaten
2 tablespoons butter
1 tablespoon lemon juice
2 egg whites, stiffly beaten (but not dry)

Sift flour with salt and sugar into mixing bowl. Combine milk with egg yolks, stir into flour, and beat with a wire whisk until smooth. Blend in butter and lemon juice,* then gently fold in egg whites. Let stand 15 to 20 minutes before using.

TO DEEP-FRY FRITTERS: Heat bland vegetable oil in deep heavy pan to 365°F. Use a sufficient quantity to cover fritters, but, to avoid splattering, fill pan no more than 3 to 4 inches from rim. If you don't have a deep-fat thermometer, use a small cube of bread to test the temperature. (The bread cube will brown in 35 seconds when oil is at 365°F.) Fry fritters, a few at a time, for 4 to 5 minutes, or until a light golden brown. Remove with slotted spoon and drain on paper towel.

NOTE: Do keep temperature of oil at prescribed level. If too low, your light and airy fritters will become heavy and indigestible; if too high, they will brown before centers are cooked. Do not pierce while cooking or they will become soggy and oil-filled.

APPLE FRITTERS

Peel and cut 2 or 3 large apples into thin ¼- to ½-inch slices. Sprinkle with sugar, lemon juice, and cinnamon. Dip in fritter batter and fry in deep hot fat until lightly browned. Drain on paper towels. Sprinkle with confectioners' sugar if desired.

CHERRY FRITTERS

Drain well 1 cup canned, pitted Bing cherries. Pat dry and stir into fritter batter; drop by spoonfuls into hot deep fat.

* Recipe can be made ahead to this point.

Fry until well puffed and brown. Drain on paper towels and sprinkle with confectioners' sugar.

PINEAPPLE FRITTERS

Peel and cut a pineapple into ¼-inch slices. Cut each slice into quarters. Sprinkle with sugar. Let stand 1 hour. Drain well, dip into fritter batter, and fry until delicately browned. Drain on paper toweling. Sprinkle with granulated sugar. Run under hot broiler to glaze.

CORN FRITTERS

Cut enough fresh corn from the cob to make ⅔ cup of kernels. Substitute any milk from the corn for the equivalent quantity of milk in basic fritter recipe. Make fritter batter, stir in corn; drop by spoonfuls into deep hot fat and fry until golden brown.

RICE FRITTERS

    1 cup well-cooked long-grain rice
    3 eggs
    ½ cup flour
    1 teaspoon baking powder
    corn oil
    confectioners' sugar

Place rice in mixing bowl, mash with fork. Blend in eggs, flour, and baking powder. Mix to a smooth batter. Drop batter by spoonfuls into hot oil. Fry, a few at a time, until a deep golden brown, 4 to 5 minutes. Remove with slotted spoon. Drain on paper towel. Dust lightly with confectioners' sugar. Serve with maple syrup, tart jelly, or jam.

CALAS TOUT CHAUD
(RAISED RICE FRITTERS)
SERVES SIX

½ cup rice
1 teaspoon salt
3 cups water
½ cake compressed yeast or ½ package dry yeast
½ cup lukewarm water
3 eggs, beaten
¼ cup sugar
4 tablespoons flour
½ teaspoon nutmeg
½ teaspoon vanilla
corn oil
½ cup confectioners' sugar

Boil rice in water with salt until very soft and almost dry. Mash to a smooth paste (or purée in a blender). Dissolve the yeast in warm water and stir into rice; cover lightly with a clean cloth or paper towel. Set aside to rise 12 hours or overnight. Stir in the beaten eggs, blend well, then add the sugar, flour, nutmeg, and vanilla. Beat until quite thick and smooth. (If batter seems thin, add a little more flour—1 or 2 tablespoons.) Drop by spoonfuls into deep hot corn oil. Fry until lightly browned. Drain on paper towels or brown paper. Sprinkle liberally with confectioners' sugar. Serve hot with freshly made coffee.

Fish for Breakfast

On a cold foggy morning, say the English, kippers and tea are an extremely comforting thought.

The tea should be a proper English breakfast brew, quite strong and very hot, in a pot—no tea bags, please—and remember that "unless the water be boiling and the teapot hot, a proper cup of tea cannot be got." The kippers? "Cook them any number of ways, love," advise the English. Pop them in the oven with a little milk and cream or fry them up nicely with butter on top of the stove.

What are they? If you don't know, we'll tell you. Kippers are literally smoked herring. However, the British often apply the word to any breakfast fish, just as we might say, "It's time for ham and eggs," and then order some other breakfast food, such as waffles and creamed chipped beef.

To many Americans, kippers might seem like hearty fare for breakfast. But almost all fish, whether broiled, sautéed, or fried, make a wonderful main dish for a late and ample brunch. Serve with potatoes crisp from the pan; add sliced tomatoes· or baked fruit, and toasted scones, hot biscuits, butter, and jam. Mouth-watering! Send your husband out with rod and reel and you get out the pan.

BROILED KIPPERS
FOR EACH SERVING

1 kipper (smoked herring)
melted butter
lemon juice
freshly ground black pepper

Split kippers without breaking the back skin. Place skin-side down in shallow buttered pan. Brush with melted butter. Sprinkle with lemon juice and black pepper. Broil under moderate flame for 12 to 15 minutes.

TROUT MEUNIÈRE
SERVES FOUR

8 small fresh trout
2 cups milk
½ to ¾ cup flour
1 teaspoon salt
½ teaspoon coarse-ground black pepper
vegetable oil
4 tablespoons butter
lemon slices
parsley

Clean the fish and rinse well under cold running water. Place in shallow pan, cover with milk, and let stand for 30 to 45 minutes. Remove from milk; drain but do not dry. Coat, one at a time, in flour seasoned with salt and pepper (use additional flour if needed).

Pour enough vegetable oil into deep heavy skillet to fill ½ inch deep. Heat over medium flame. Add trout and cook until golden brown on underside; turn, and brown second side. Transfer to serving platter. Pour oil from skillet and wipe dry with paper toweling; add butter and heat to sizzling. Pour over trout. Garnish dish with thin slices of lemon and sprigs of crisp fresh parsley. Serve with oven-baked potato slices.

OVEN-BAKED POTATO SLICES
SERVES FOUR

2 to 3 large Idaho potatoes
3 tablespoons melted butter
salt to taste

Scrub potatoes clean, pat dry, and cut into uniform ¼-inch slices (discard end pieces). Dip each slice in melted butter. Place in single layer, not touching, on greased cookie sheet or aluminum foil. Bake at 400°F. until tender. Run under hot broiler to brown surface. Sprinkle with salt and serve.

BROILED SHAD ROE
AU BEURRE NOIR
SERVES TWO

2 shad roe
salted water
cold water
juice of ½ lemon
4 tablespoons butter
salt and pepper to taste
1 teaspoon white wine vinegar
1 tablespoon chopped parsley

Simmer shad roe 15 minutes in salted water to cover, with lemon juice. Remove with slotted spatula. Transfer to cold water for 5 minutes, drain, and pat dry.

Melt butter in saucepan, sprinkle roe with salt and pepper, place on an oiled rack, and brush surface with butter. Broil approximately 4 inches from flame for 5 minutes. Turn, again brush with butter. Broil until surface is a light golden brown. Place on serving platter or plates. Cook remaining butter in saucepan over high heat until it turns quite dark. Stir in vinegar and parsley. Pour over shad roe and serve with crisp bacon and scrambled eggs.

HADDOCK FILLETS IN OATMEAL
SERVES SIX TO EIGHT

¾ to 1 cup oatmeal
1 egg
¼ cup milk
1 tablespoon salad oil
½ teaspoon salt
6 to 8 haddock fillets
½ cup flour
oil
2 tablespoons butter
lemon wedges

Blend oatmeal in electric blender to cracker crumb consistency, or place between two sheets of waxed paper and use rolling pin to crush fine. Set aside. Beat egg with milk, salad oil, and salt. Wipe fillets dry; dip first in flour, then in egg mixture, then roll in oatmeal.

Heat ¼ inch oil in heavy skillet, and sauté the fillets, turning once, until well browned on both sides. Transfer to serving platter. Pour off oil in skillet, wipe clean with paper toweling, add butter, and heat to sizzling. Pour over fillets. Top each with a lemon wedge and serve with country-fried potatoes.

COUNTRY-FRIED POTATOES
SERVES SIX TO EIGHT

3 to 4 medium to large Idaho potatoes
2 tablespoons salad oil
1 tablespoon butter
salt and pepper to taste

Scrub potatoes clean, pat dry, and slice thin. Place in a bowl of ice water for 20 to 30 minutes. Drain, pat dry. Heat oil and butter in heavy skillet. Add potatoes, cover, and cook over low flame until bottom layer of potatoes is brown (approximately 25 minutes). Turn, sprinkle with salt and pepper, and brown the other side.

SAUTÉED SMELTS WITH DEVILED BUTTER SAUCE
SERVES FOUR

2 pounds smelts
salt and pepper to taste
flour
butter and oil
4 tablespoons butter
2 tablespoons lemon juice
1 tablespoon prepared mustard
3 tablespoons Worcestershire sauce
2 or 3 dashes Tabasco sauce
lemon slices and parsley

Sprinkle smelts with salt and pepper. Roll in flour. Sauté in large heavy skillet in half butter and half oil until crisp and browned. Transfer to serving platter. Pour off oil from pan and wipe clean with paper toweling. Add 4 tablespoons butter and cook until sizzling. Stir in remaining ingredients, stir to blend. Pour over fish. Garnish platter with lemon slices and parsley. Serve with potato sticks.

KEDGEREE
SERVES SIX

>1 pound cooked flaked salmon
>3 cups cooked rice
>3 hard-cooked eggs, cut into thin wedges
>1 teaspoon fresh lime juice
>¼ teaspoon grated nutmeg
>¼ teaspoon coriander
>¼ teaspoon powdered ginger
>1 teaspoon salt
>½ teaspoon pepper
>¾ cup cream
>6 tablespoons butter

Mix together the salmon, rice, and eggs. Stir in the lime juice and seasonings, the cream, and 3 tablespoons butter. Pour into a well-greased ovenproof casserole. Dot with remaining butter and bake in preheated 350°F. oven for 30 to 40 minutes. Serve from casserole.

PARSLEY CODFISH CAKES
SERVES FOUR

>2 cups cooked flaked codfish
>2 cups mashed potatoes
>1 teaspoon minced onion
>¼ cup minced parsley
>3 tablespoons melted butter
>3 eggs, beaten
>½ cup milk
>fine dry bread crumbs
>oil and butter

Mix together first 7 ingredients. Shape into small cakes. Roll in bread crumbs. Chill thoroughly 2 hours or longer. Fill frying pan to ¼ inch with half oil, half butter; heat. Add cakes and cook, turning once, over medium flame, until nicely browned. Drain briefly on paper toweling before serving.

Hot Breads,
Biscuits, and Buns

With so many freshly baked breads and frozen baked goods available these days, it's no wonder that the homemade variety has gone out of style. But what a pity! Of all the breakfast aromas, the smell of bread baking in an oven is still the most tantalizing.

Here are recipes for yeast breads and quick breads, biscuits, rolls, muffins, and coffee cake, too. You can achieve the same homey "come down to breakfast" fragrance even when you prepare them ahead, freeze, and then bake or reheat them.

BISHOP'S BREAD

    3 cups packaged biscuit mix
    1 cup sugar
    1 egg
    1 tablespoon grated orange rind
    1½ cups orange juice
    3 tablespoons salad oil
    ½ cup wheat germ
    ¼ cup seedless raisins
    ¼ cup halved candied cherries
    ¼ cup chopped nuts

Combine biscuit mix and sugar in large mixing bowl. Combine egg, orange rind, and juice; add salad oil. Add to mixing bowl and beat hard until mixture is smooth. Stir in wheat germ, raisins, cherries, and nuts. Turn into greased and waxed paper-lined loaf pan. Bake at 350°F. approximately 1 hour. Cool before removing from pan.

LOUISIANA CORN BREAD

    2 cups white cornmeal
    1 teaspoon salt
    3 teaspoons baking powder
    3 eggs, well beaten
    1 tablespoon melted butter
    1½ cups milk
    1 cup cold boiled rice

Sift cornmeal, salt, and baking powder into mixing bowl. Stir in the eggs, butter, milk, and rice. Beat well. Pour into a shallow, well-greased baking pan. Bake at 375°F. for 30 minutes (or until firm). Cut into squares, butter while hot, and serve with strawberry jam.

"QUICK DELIVERY" BREAD

    1 loaf firm unsliced white bread
    ¼ pound (1 stick) butter

Cut crust from the two sides and the ends of loaf, leaving top and bottom crust. Cut loaf in two, lengthwise. Divide each half into 6 or 8 squares, cutting to—but not through—bottom crust. Place each half on foil in 400°F. oven until hot and lightly toasted. While bread heats, melt butter; when sizzling pour slowly over hot bread, letting it run down between squares. Place under broiler a half-minute. Then serve piping hot from napkin-lined bread basket.

Here are three rich sweet breads—to make any time. Slice, then toast or serve warm from the oven.

PRUNE AND WALNUT BREAD

½ cup butter
1 cup sugar
2 eggs
1½ cups flour
1 teaspoon baking soda
1 teaspoon salt
½ teaspoon cinnamon
½ teaspoon nutmeg
½ teaspoon allspice
2 teaspoons baking powder
¾ cup buttermilk
1 cup chopped walnuts
1 cup stewed prune pulp
2 tablespoons prune juice
confectioners' sugar (optional)

Cream butter with sugar; add eggs and blend well. Sift together flour, soda, salt, cinnamon, nutmeg, allspice, and baking powder. Add alternately with buttermilk to egg mixture. Stir in walnuts, prune pulp, and prune juice. Pour into buttered and floured shallow square pan. Bake at 350°F. for 25 to 30 minutes. Cool, turn out onto cake rack. Dust with confectioners' sugar if desired.

BANANA BREAD

½ cup butter
1 cup sugar

1 cup mashed banana pulp (approximately 3 to
4 bananas)
2 eggs, lightly beaten
2 cups flour
1 teaspoon salt
1 teaspoon baking soda
¼ cup sour milk
½ teaspoon vanilla

Cream the butter with the sugar; add banana pulp, blend, and beat in eggs. Sift in flour with salt and baking soda. Add sour milk and vanilla. Blend well, pour into 12-inch loaf pan. Bake at 350°F. for 50 to 55 minutes, or until firm and lightly browned. Leave in pan 5 minutes, then turn out onto cake rack to cool slightly before cutting.

APPLESAUCE BREAD

½ cup butter
1 cup sugar
2 eggs
1½ cups canned applesauce
2 cups sifted flour
1 teaspoon baking powder
1 teaspoon salt
½ teaspoon nutmeg
½ teaspoon vanilla
1 cup chopped nutmeats
½ cup raisins

Cream together the butter and sugar; add eggs one at a time, beating after each addition. Stir in remaining ingredients. Blend. Bake in well-greased loaf pan at 350°F. for 50 to 55 minutes or until firm.

BREAKFAST ROLLS
MAKES FOUR TO FIVE DOZEN ROLLS

1 cake compressed yeast or 1 package dry
  granular yeast
3 tablespoons sugar
¼ cup warm water
1 cup milk
½ cup soft butter (at room temperature)
1 teaspoon salt
2 eggs, lightly beaten
4⅓ cups flour

Dissolve the yeast and 1 tablespoon sugar in the warm water.
Scald the milk in large saucepan, then add butter, remaining
sugar, and salt. Cool to lukewarm, add dissolved yeast and
eggs; blend. Sift in flour gradually and mix to a smooth
dough. Turn out onto lightly floured board. Knead until
smooth and elastic. Place in greased bowl. Let rise in warm
place until double in bulk. Cut down, cover bowl with foil.
Refrigerate 24 hours or longer. When ready to use, pinch off
the desired portion.

For plain breakfast rolls, roll out to ⅓-inch thickness.
Spread with soft butter and cut into rounds; fold each round
over so edges meet. Press edges together. Place in rows, close
together in greased pan. Let rise for 1 to 1½ hours or until
double in bulk. Bake in preheated 400°F. oven for 20 to 25
minutes or until lightly browned.

And a Few Ways to Make Them Interesting:

CINNAMON ROLLS

Prepare dough for basic breakfast rolls. Roll out, spread with
butter, and sprinkle with ¾ cup sugar and 2 teaspoons cin-

74

namon, blended together. Roll up as a jelly roll, wrap in
waxed paper, and chill. Slice and bake at 350°F. until nicely
browned.

HOT CROSS BUNS

Increase sugar in basic recipe to ½ cup and fold 1 cup mixed
candied fruit and 1 cup raisins into dough mixture before
adding flour. Proceed as directed for basic rolls. When baked,
cool and ice top lightly with plain confectioners' sugar icing.

ORANGE BISCUIT ROLLS
MAKES ABOUT TWENTY-FOUR SMALL BISCUITS

    2 cups flour
    3 teaspoons baking powder
    ½ teaspoon salt
    4 tablespoons very cold hard butter
    1 egg, slightly beaten
    ¼ to ½ cup milk
    3 tablespoons soft butter (at room temperature)
    ½ cup bitter Seville marmalade

Sift flour, baking powder, and salt into mixing bowl. Cut in
butter until mixture resembles coarse-ground cornmeal. Add
egg and enough milk to mix to a stiff dough. Turn out on a
well-floured board and knead lightly.

Roll out into an oblong sheet, approximately ¼ inch thick.
Spread first with soft butter, then marmalade; fold over, and
cut with knife into finger-length, 1-inch strips. Seal edges by
pressing lightly with fingers. Place, not touching, on flat tray.
Cover with foil. Chill in refrigerator 2 hours or longer (will
keep in refrigerator up to 1 week). To serve, bake at 425°F.
until a light golden brown (15 to 20 minutes).

KUCHEN ROLL

Divide basic breakfast roll dough into thirds. Roll each third out to ½-inch thickness. Spread with soft butter and sprinkle with brown sugar, cinnamon, chopped nuts, and raisins. Roll up jelly-roll fashion and place in greased loaf pans. Let rise until double in bulk. Bake in preheated oven for 30 to 35 minutes, or until firm and lightly browned.

HONEY PECAN STICKY BUNS

Roll out basic breakfast roll dough to ⅓-inch thickness. Spread with soft butter. Sprinkle with brown sugar and chopped pecans. Roll up jelly-roll fashion. Cut into 1-inch slices. Grease a shallow loaf pan with shortening (not butter); cover shortening with a thin layer of honey. Sprinkle honey generously with brown sugar and chopped pecans. Arrange rolls close together, cutside down, over mixture. Let rise in warm place until double in bulk (1 to 1½ hours). Bake in preheated 400°F. oven for 25 to 30 minutes.

CROISSANTS
MAKES TWENTY-FOUR CROISSANTS

> 2 envelopes active dry yeast
> ¼ cup warm water (105°F. to 115°F.)
> 5 cups flour
> 1 teaspoon salt
> 1 tablespoon sugar
> ¾ cup milk
> 1 cup (½ pound) butter (at room temperature)
> 1 egg yolk beaten with 1 tablespoon water

Sprinkle yeast over warm water in mixing bowl. Stir until dissolved. Add 1 cup flour. Blend and stir to a smooth ball.

Cover with foil and let rise in a warm place* until double in bulk. Sift remaining flour, salt, and sugar into second bowl. Stir in milk and mix it to a smooth dough. Combine with yeast mixture. Cover and let rest 20 minutes. Roll out on a floured board. Cover half the dough generously with some of the soft butter, fold second half over buttered half, and roll out again. Repeat until all butter has been used (about 4 "folds"). Then refrigerate dough until thoroughly chilled (about 1 hour). Roll out about ⅛ inch thick and cut into 6-inch squares. Cut each square diagonally, making two triangles from each. Roll each loosely, starting from longest side of triangle. Shape each into a crescent. Place on lightly floured baking sheet, cover with a towel, and let rise in a warm place for about 1 hour (or until double in bulk). Brush with egg yolk and water mixture. Bake in preheated 400°F. oven for 5 minutes, then reduce heat to 350°F., and bake for 15 to 20 minutes or until lightly browned.

BRIOCHE
SERVES TEN TO TWELVE

> ½ cup warm water (105°F. to 115°F.)
> 1 package active dry yeast
> 3 tablespoons sugar
> 2 teaspoons salt
> ½ pound butter (at room temperature)
> 8 eggs (at room temperature)
> 5 cups all-purpose flour
> 1 egg yolk beaten with 1 tablespoon water

If you have a thermometer, check the temperature of the water—it does make a difference. And make sure, by checking the date on the package, that the yeast is really fresh.

---

* To let rise in warm place, heat oven at 200°F. for 5 minutes. Open oven door and wait 5 minutes before placing bowl of dough on center rack. Leave oven door open. Temperature of oven should be about 85°F.

Sprinkle yeast over warm water in large bowl of electric mixer. Stir until yeast is dissolved. Add sugar, salt, butter, 3 cups flour, and 6 eggs. Beat at medium speed for 4 minutes, occasionally scraping beaters and sides of bowl with rubber scraper. Add remaining flour and eggs. Beat at low speed 2 minutes longer (the dough will be soft). Cover bowl with foil, and let rise in a warm place* until double in bulk (about 2 hours). Beat dough down, then refrigerate covered with foil overnight.

Next morning, grease a 2-quart brioche mold† generously. Shape ¼ of the dough on a lightly floured board into a small ball. Shape remaining dough, again on floured board, into a ball about 6 inches in diameter. Place in greased brioche mold. With your fingers, make an indentation and place smaller ball of dough in center. Cover with towel and set in warm place, free from drafts, until double in bulk (about 2 hours). Brush surface lightly with beaten egg yolk and water. (Use pastry brush and a light hand; do not allow yolk mixture to run between brioche and its cap.) Bake at 400°F. for 55 to 60 minutes. Cover top loosely with foil for last 30 minutes of baking.

Let stand on wire rack 15 minutes before taking from pan. Loosen sides carefully with knife; remove to round platter. Cut in wedges and serve warm at the breakfast table.

HOT BISCUITS
MAKES TWELVE LARGE OR TWENTY-FOUR SMALL BISCUITS

   2 cups sifted flour
   1 teaspoon salt
   3 tablespoons baking powder

---

* To let rise in warm place, heat oven at 200°F. for 5 minutes. Open oven door and wait 5 minutes before placing bowl of dough on center rack. Leave oven door open. Temperature of oven should be about 85°F.
† Conventional brioche molds are bowl-shaped and often fluted. You will find them in shops that feature gourmet cooking equipment. Brioche dough may also be baked in French soufflé molds, loaf pans, or muffin tins.

⅓ cup shortening
¾ cup milk
1 egg
1 tablespoon melted butter
cold milk

Sift flour, salt, and baking powder into mixing bowl. Cut in shortening until mixture resembles coarse-ground cornmeal. Mix milk with egg, add all at once, and mix to a smooth dough. Turn out onto floured board. Knead lightly, roll out about ½ inch thick, and brush with melted butter. Fold dough in half, roll out once more, and cut with biscuit cutter. Place on ungreased cookie sheet. Brush surfaces with cold milk. If time allows, refrigerate until well chilled. Bake at 450°F. for 10 to 15 minutes or until lightly browned.

And a Few Ways to Make Them Interesting:

BACON BISCUITS

Add ¼ cup crumbled cooked bacon to basic recipe.

CHEESE BISCUITS

Add ½ cup grated sharp cheese to dry ingredients.

HERB BISCUITS

Add 1 teaspoon mixed herbs to dry ingredients.

CINNAMON BISCUITS

Add ½ teaspoon cinnamon, ¼ teaspoon nutmeg, and 1 teaspoon sugar to dry ingredients. Fold ½ cup seeded raisins into basic batter.

PLAIN MUFFINS
MAKES TWELVE LARGE OR TWENTY-FOUR SMALL MUFFINS

2 cups flour
1 teaspoon salt
4 teaspoons baking powder
2 teaspoons sugar
2 eggs, well beaten
1 cup milk
¼ teaspoon vanilla
3 tablespoons melted butter

Sift dry ingredients into mixing bowl. Mix together eggs, milk, vanilla, and butter. Combine the two mixtures, blend lightly. Fill well-greased muffin tins ¾ full. Bake at 425°F. for 20 to 25 minutes.

And a Few Ways to Make Them Interesting:

DATE-NUT MUFFINS

Blend ¼ cup chopped pitted dates and ¼ cup chopped pecans to sifted dry ingredients.

BLUEBERRY MUFFINS

Fold 1 cup fresh, canned, or (completely thawed) frozen blueberries into batter.

ORANGE MUFFINS

Add 2 tablespoons grated orange rind to batter.

SPICY MUFFINS

Add ⅛ teaspoon nutmeg and ¼ teaspoon each cinnamon and ginger to dry ingredients. Sprinkle tops generously with sugar and cinnamon before baking.

HAM MUFFINS

Eliminate vanilla, and add ½ cup finely diced lean cooked ham to batter.

ALMOND MUFFINS

Substitute almond extract for vanilla; fold ½ cup chopped blanched almonds into batter.

PINEAPPLE MUFFINS

Add ½ cup chopped, well-drained, canned or fresh pineapple to batter.

GINGER MUFFINS

Add ¼ teaspoon powdered ginger and ½ cup chopped candied ginger to dry ingredients.

JELLY MUFFINS

Before baking, make a small depression in the center of each muffin and fill with ¼ teaspoon of any tart jelly.

CORN MUFFINS
MAKES TWELVE LARGE OR TWENTY-FOUR SMALL MUFFINS

1½ cups yellow cornmeal
½ cup sifted flour
1 tablespoon baking powder
1 tablespoon sugar
1 teaspoon salt
3 eggs, lightly beaten
1⅓ cups milk
¼ teaspoon vanilla
4 tablespoons melted butter

Combine first five ingredients in mixing bowl. Stir in eggs and milk, blend, and add vanilla and butter. Butter and heat muffin tins, pour in batter, and bake at 400°F. for 20 to 25 minutes or until lightly browned.

POPOVERS
MAKES ABOUT TWELVE POPOVERS

1 cup flour
½ teaspoon salt
1 cup milk
3 eggs, beaten
2 tablespoons melted butter

Heavily grease popover pans or ovenproof glass custard cups with corn oil. Place in 400°F. oven for 10 minutes. Mix flour and salt. Add milk to eggs. Combine the two mixtures and blend until smooth. Add butter and beat with wire whisk a full 2 minutes—or place all ingredients in order listed in electric blender and blend at high speed until smooth. Pour batter into hot popover pans or custard cups. Bake 20 minutes in preheated 450°F. oven. Reduce heat to 350°F. and bake 30 minutes longer. (Do not peek for the first 30 minutes.) Puncture top of each popover with fork to allow steam to escape. Turn off heat and return them to oven for 5 minutes before serving.

BLACK TREACLE SCONES
MAKES TWENTY SCONES

    4 cups flour
    1 tablespoon sugar
    ½ teaspoon cinnamon
    ¼ teaspoon nutmeg
    ¼ teaspoon ginger
    3 tablespoons butter
    3 tablespoons black treacle (dark molasses)
    1 cup buttermilk
    1 egg, beaten

Sift dry ingredients into mixing bowl and stir in butter, molasses, and buttermilk. Mix to a soft dough. Turn out onto lightly floured board and divide dough into four quarters. Roll out into thick ovals. Cut each oval into four wedges. Brush with beaten egg. Bake on greased cookie sheet (or aluminum foil) at 400°F. for 15 to 20 minutes or until lightly browned.

QUICK-MIX COFFEE CAKE

    2 cups packaged biscuit mix
    1 cup chopped walnuts
    ½ cup brown sugar, firmly packed
    ½ cup milk
    1 egg, slightly beaten
    3 tablespoons melted butter
    ⅓ cup flour
    ¼ cup sugar
    ½ teaspoon cinnamon
    ¼ cup melted butter

Blend together the biscuit mix, half the walnuts, and the sugar. Add milk, egg, and butter. Stir only until blended. Pour into well-greased (8-inch) square loaf pan. Place remaining ingredients in same bowl in which batter was mixed. Blend with your fingers until it forms small crumbs. Sprinkle over top of batter. Bake in preheated 400°F. oven for 25 to 30 minutes. Serve hot or reheated but not cold.

DOUGHNUTS
MAKES ABOUT THIRTY-SIX SMALL DOUGHNUTS

2 eggs
1 cup sugar
1 teaspoon baking soda
⅔ cup sour milk
3 tablespoons melted butter
3½ cups flour
1 teaspoon salt
1 teaspoon baking powder
½ teaspoon cinnamon
½ teaspoon nutmeg
¼ teaspoon ginger
confectioners' sugar or granulated sugar and
    cinnamon

Beat the eggs until light; add the sugar. Dissolve the soda in the sour milk, stir into eggs and sugar, add butter, and blend well. Sift flour with salt, baking powder, cinnamon, nutmeg, and ginger; combine with egg mixture. Beat until smooth. Shape into ball (if dough is not thick enough add a little, but just a little, flour). Cover and chill thoroughly. Roll out on floured board to about ¼-inch thickness. Cut out with small doughnut cutter. Fry in deep hot fat (370°F.). Turn only once, carefully; if pierced, doughnuts become heavy and fat-soaked. Cook only a few at a time. Keep fat at even temperature. Drain on paper toweling. Roll in confectioners' sugar or in granulated sugar and cinnamon.

The Perfect
Morning Brew

Coffee

Let the fragrance of freshly brewed coffee waft out of the kitchen and up the stairs, and even the laziest dawdler will hurry down to breakfast.

A perfect cup of coffee? Here are the basic rules:

BUY COFFEE IN THE BEAN, FRESHLY ROASTED. *Most large cities, and quite a few small ones too, can boast of at least one shop where freshly roasted coffee beans may be purchased. You may also roast your own green beans. Simply spread beans out on a large baking sheet and "roast" in a low oven (300°F.). Stir often. Roast until well browned. Mmmmmm, the aroma alone is worth the trouble.*

BUY THE VERY BEST, MOST EXPENSIVE BLEND OF BEANS YOUR MERCHANT FEATURES. *The finer the coffee the less you need use to make a strong but clear brew.*

GRIND YOUR OWN FRESHLY ROASTED BEANS. *Aroma and freshness are retained in the bean but quickly lost after grinding. Small electric coffee grinders are inexpensive and effective. You will find them in housewares departments, hardware stores, and gourmet shops. Coffee beans may also be ground in an electric blender.*

GRIND ONLY THE AMOUNT YOU PLAN TO USE IMMEDIATELY. *Whole beans remain fresh longer than ground coffee.*

SELECT ANY KIND OF POT, BUT KEEP IT CLEAN, CLEAN, CLEAN. *A "stained" pot is a pot that has been inadequately washed. The stain is simply coffee that has been allowed to remain in the pot. This coffee residue becomes rancid and affects the flavor each time you brew "fresh." Wash the pot after each use with mild soap and warm water. Rinse in scalding water. Dry thoroughly before putting it away.*

SERVE FRESHLY MADE COFFEE ONLY. *Do not reheat—ever. Once made, keep it hot (but do not allow it to boil) on an asbestos pad or in a pan of water over low heat.*

ALWAYS MEASURE COFFEE AND WATER ACCURATELY. DON'T GUESS. *Exact proportions of coffee to water cannot be given accurately. It depends on the strength of the bean, how it is ground, and the type of pot used. You will find that less coffee is needed if you use a finely ground, top-grade blend, and a drip or vacuum-style pot. Start by using 1 level tablespoon of coffee to each cup of water, then adjust to suit your taste, as well as the type of pot and coffee used.*

For a special breakfast, there's special coffee. But then, special coffee makes any breakfast special, and takes no special skill.

Most people find the following coffees particularly good. We like to serve them after breakfast rather as one would a dessert, and then sit around the breakfast table for talk and more talk till noon.

ESPRESSO

For the real thing, invest in a small electric espresso machine and follow the manufacturer's instructions. For a reasonably good imitation, brew finely ground dark-roast coffee in a drip or vacuum pot. Serve in demitasse cups with a twist of lemon peel. Black, of course, and sweetened to taste. A teaspoon of cognac or blended whiskey adds greatly to the flavor.

CAPUCCINO

Make coffee in an electric espresso machine, or brew it in a drip pot from finely ground dark-roast beans. Mix with equal parts hot (but not boiling) milk. Add a teaspoon of sugar to each cup. Top with thick, thick cream sprinkled with nutmeg. (If cream is not heavy enough to float on surface of coffee, beat until thick but not stiff.)

NOTE: Electric espresso machines may be found in housewares departments and gourmet shops. Instructions for use come with your purchase.

CHOCOLATE RUM COFFEE

To each freshly made, very hot cup of coffee add 1 teaspoon semisweet, finely ground chocolate and 1 teaspoon dark rum. Serve black or with whipped cream.

CAFÉ AU LAIT

Pour coffee (brewed from finely ground dark-roast beans) and hot (but not boiling) milk simultaneously into cup. Sweeten to taste.

VIENNESE COFFEE

Cover each cup of very hot, clear, strong, and freshly made coffee with sweetened whipped cream. Sprinkle with grated orange rind or nutmeg or both.

MORNING ICED COFFEE

Brew coffee double-strength. Freeze in ice-cube trays. Fill tall glasses with frozen cubes. Pour in freshly made hot coffee. (A spoon placed in the glass will keep it from cracking.) Serve with sugar and heavy cream.

BOILED COFFEE
SERVES THIRTY-FIVE TO FORTY PEOPLE

    1 pound medium-grind coffee
    1 egg
    10 quarts boiling water

Mix coffee with egg and enough cold water to moisten thoroughly. Place in finely woven cheesecloth bag. Drop into boiling water in large pot. Boil for 10 minutes. Let stand about 3 minutes before serving.

Tea

The English claim that we Americans prefer coffee simply because we do not know how to make proper tea. We might say the same in reverse of coffee and the English, but we tactfully refrain.

Unless you have experienced the downright satisfaction of a cup of bracing, warming, English breakfast tea, you have not had tea at its best, at its peak of perfection.

TO MAKE A PERFECT CUP OF TEA: Fill teapot with boiling water. Bring a second pan of water to a full boil. Pour water from teapot, add 1 teaspoon tea for each cup of water, and pour freshly boiled water directly over tea. Cover pot; allow to steep for about 3 minutes. Stir once; steep for 2 minutes more. Serve with lemon or rich milk (not cream) and sugar.

THE GOURMET'S CUP OF TEA: Brew tea as per basic instructions, but use bottled water in the brewing. Sweeten tea with brandy. Serve with paper-thin slices of lemon.

However, this is only half the story. Brewed tea can be only as good as the tea used in its brewing. So start by buying the best. Shop for tea as you would for fine wines. The flavor spectrum is just as wide. Some teas are sophisticated; others are simple. The principal classifications—black, Oolong, and green—are all available in this country. Try smooth and delicate Keemun, sometimes referred to as the burgundy of Chinese teas, which is also sold under the name English Breakfast tea; or Formosa Oolong, which has a more intense taste and a special fruity flavor, and has been called the champagne of tea. Sample Earl Grey and Darjeeling, Jasmine, Assam, and Ceylon, as well as any number of other blends. In other words, taste-test until you find a tea to please your palate.

You'll discover more than one and you'll have real pleasure in the finding, too.

Breakfast à Deux

Doctors prescribe it, nutritionists insist on it, and the most militant dieters attest to its worth. Perhaps that is the flaw. Everything else that is good for you has a way of being unpleasant, so how could breakfast be such sheer delight? Yet it is. In fact, breakfast is the pleasantest of all meals for a twosome—a time to forget last night's quarrel, a time for a fresh start, a new beginning.

Sweet Start for a Cold Morning

Easy Apple Breakfast Pie
Canadian Bacon
Coffee

EASY APPLE BREAKFAST PIE

6 to 8 slices white bread
½ cup (1 stick) melted butter
6 to 8 apples, peeled, cored, and diced
½ cup sugar
½ teaspoon cinnamon
½ teaspoon nutmeg

Remove crust from bread; cut each slice into three strips. Dip strips in melted butter and use them to line bottom and sides of a shallow square or oblong baking dish. Fill with apples and sprinkle with the sugar, plus cinnamon and nutmeg to taste. Pour any remaining butter over surface. Bake in a preheated 400°F. oven until apples are tender. Serve warm, with thick cream to pour over.

Summer Patio Breakfast

Grapefruit Shells*
Pain Perdu
Skillet Bacon with Brown Sugar
Sautéed Bananas*
Coffee

PAIN PERDU

½ to ⅔ cup milk
½ teaspoon sugar
2 or 3 drops orange-flower water
8 slices day-old bread (crusts removed)
2 eggs, separated
dash of nutmeg
butter and corn oil, half and half
confectioners' sugar

Combine milk, sugar, and orange-flower water. Pour over bread slices placed in a single layer in shallow pan. Soak while you beat egg yolks until light, adding nutmeg to yolks. Beat whites until stiff but still quite moist. Fold in yolks. Remove bread from milk, press lightly, dip into beaten eggs, and sauté the slices in mixture of half butter, half corn oil until

* Recipe in this book.

92

a crisp golden brown on each side. Remove to serving plate, dust with confectioners' sugar, and serve with molasses or dark cane syrup.

SKILLET BACON WITH BROWN SUGAR

½ pound bacon
1 tablespoon brown sugar

Place bacon in cold skillet and cook over low heat, pressing fat from slices with a spatula to prevent curling. Pour off drippings and turn occasionally. When almost crisp, sprinkle with brown sugar. Cook until sugar has melted. Drain on paper towels and serve.

Paris Remembered

Sliced Bananas with Cream and Brown Sugar
French-Style Poached Eggs
on Smithfield Ham Toast
Coffee

FRENCH-STYLE POACHED EGGS ON SMITHFIELD HAM TOAST

4 eggs
1 teaspoon vinegar
dash of salt
4 slices toast
Smithfield ham spread

Fill a large skillet with 3 inches of water. Add vinegar and salt; bring to boil. With a long-handled spoon, stir the water

93

rapidly in one direction to form a hollow whirlpool and slip an egg into its center. The white of the egg will form around the yolk, giving a puffy round effect to the egg. Cook one egg at a time. As each is cooked, transfer to a bowl of hot salted water to keep warm while you prepare the remainder Spread toast generously with Smithfield ham spread. Top each slice with poached egg.

Sunday Brunch for Two

Well-Chilled and Seasoned Tomato Juice
Chicken Livers and Apples on Toast Points
Scrambled Eggs with Fresh Herbs
Cinnamon Rolls*
Coffee

CHICKEN LIVERS AND APPLES ON TOAST POINTS

½ pound chicken livers
¼ cup flour
½ teaspoon salt
½ teaspoon coarse-ground black pepper
2 tablespoons butter
1 Italian onion, chopped
1 teaspoon Worcestershire sauce
1 tart apple, sliced
1 teaspoon sugar

Dredge the chicken livers in flour seasoned with salt and pepper. Brown slowly in half of the butter. Melt remaining butter in separate pan; in it sauté the onion until limp but not brown. Use spatula or slotted spoon to remove onion; place on top of chicken livers and add Worcestershire sauce.

* Recipe in this book.

Cover pan and cook over very low heat. Sauté the apple slices in the same pan in which onion was cooked, until just tender; sprinkle with sugar. Cover and cook until sugar has melted. Place over onion and chicken livers and serve on toast points.

Monday Morning Gourmet

Frozen Strawberries in Fresh Orange Juice
Scrambled Eggs with Parsley and Cottage Cheese
Oven-broiled Ham Slices
Orange Biscuit Rolls*
Coffee

SCRAMBLED EGGS WITH PARSLEY AND COTTAGE CHEESE

2 tablespoons butter
4 eggs, lightly beaten
¼ cup cottage cheese
½ teaspoon salt
¼ cup chopped parsley

Melt the butter in a heavy skillet. Pour in the eggs, blend quickly with a fork, then add the cottage cheese and salt. Cook, stirring constantly, until just set. Stir in the parsley and serve.

OVEN-BROILED HAM SLICES

Place ½-inch-thick precooked ham slices on greased foil. Dot with butter or tiny strips of ham fat. Bake until thoroughly

* Recipe in this book.

95

heated. Spread with tart jelly if desired and run under broiler until jelly is melted and bubbly.

Celebration Breakfast

Fresh Strawberries Dusted with
Confectioners' Sugar
Champagne
Russian Eggs on Anchovy Toast
Coffee
Then More Coffee and Miniature Danish Pastries

RUSSIAN EGGS
ON ANCHOVY TOAST

4 eggs
4 slices of toast (crust removed)
anchovy butter (see below)
1 cup **Hollandaise** sauce (see **p.** 97)
1 small jar caviar

Poach the eggs, spread toast with anchovy butter, place 1 egg on each slice, and cover with Hollandaise sauce. Sprinkle with caviar and serve.

ANCHOVY BUTTER

3 tablespoons butter
1 tablespoon anchovy paste

Cream the butter, add the anchovy paste, and blend well.

HOLLANDAISE SAUCE

½ cup (1 stick) butter (at room temperature)
3 egg yolks
2 tablespoons lemon juice
¼ teaspoon salt

Cream the butter in top half of double boiler, beat in the egg
yolks, lemon juice, and salt with a wire whisk. Set aside at
this point, if desired, until 5 minutes before serving. Again
place over the boiling water and blend by beating rapidly
with a wire whisk. Sauce may be kept over hot, but not
boiling, water for a few minutes before serving.

Epicurean, but Quick

Stewed Prunes and Oranges
Cheese Toast with Bacon
Coffee

CHEESE TOAST WITH BACON

4 slices bacon
1 egg
¼ cup grated Cheddar cheese
1 tablespoon butter (at room temperature)
cayenne pepper
4 slices white bread

Cut each slice of bacon in half. Broil or fry until half done,
drain on paper towel, set aside. Beat the egg lightly, add the
cheese, and cream to a smooth paste. Spread the bread slices,
first with soft butter, then with the cheese mixture; sprinkle
liberally with cayenne pepper and top with the partially
cooked bacon. Broil under medium flame until cheese is
bubbly and bacon is crisp.

For Two Special People

Orange Juice
Noisettes d'Agneau
Crabapple Slices
Potato Balls
Coffee

NOISETTES D'AGNEAU

4 ¾-inch-thick lamb chops
salt and pepper to taste
4 large fresh mushroom caps
2 tablespoons butter
4 slices toast

To prepare noisettes, have your butcher bone, roll, and wrap chops in bacon. Bring to room temperature before broiling. Broil 5 minutes on each side under medium broiler flame, or until done to your taste. Season to taste with salt and pepper. While meat is broiling, sauté mushroom caps in butter (about 5 minutes) and make toast. Place noisettes on toast. Pour a little of the mushroom butter over each, and top with mushroom cap.

POTATO BALLS

2 pounds potatoes
½ cup light cream, heated
¼ cup melted butter
¼ teaspoon salt
¼ teaspoon pepper
1 egg, well beaten
½ cup fine cracker crumbs

Boil potatoes until quite soft, and peel while hot. Place in mixing bowl and add cream and melted butter. Mash thoroughly, then beat until fluffy. Season with salt and pepper. Form into small balls, roll in beaten egg, then cracker crumbs. Chill, then bake at 450°F. for 10 minutes. Or, place, not touching, on flat tray and freeze until firm. Wrap in foil and store in freezer. Bake frozen for 10 to 15 minutes at 400°F.

Brunch and Buffets

There are as many reasons to give a party as there are ways to entertain. Whether your purpose is to return invitations, to honor a special person, or just to enjoy the company of friends, no other celebration is quite as easy or as impressive as a party breakfast or mid-morning brunch.

Though there's no reason to stress the point when inviting guests, no other party is quite as inexpensive. Due to the early hour, cocktails are limited, and even the finest breakfast foods are less costly than the equivalent fare for an equally festive luncheon or dinner.

While it's true that many breakfast foods must be cooked and served at the last minute, your menu need include no more than one dish in this category; the rest may be prepared ahead and reheated. Since breakfast is usually an informal meal you will need little or no help to serve.

This is the time when you can really make use of your chafing dish, hot plate, and portable oven. Serve buffet style; let your guests help themselves, then relax and enjoy your own party.

Here are six buffet menus we have found successful over the years. They range from an informal Texas breakfast cookout to a very formal wedding breakfast.

Texas Breakfast Cookout

Bourbon Old-Fashioneds
Pitcher of Fresh Grapefruit
and Orange Juice, Half 'n' Half
Skillet Ham and Eggs
Home-Fried Potatoes
Herb Biscuits*   Fig Jam
Honey Butter
Sugar-Dusted Doughnuts*
Coffee

SKILLET HAM AND EGGS
SERVES SIX

    6 slices boiled or baked ham (approximately ¼
       inch thick)
    12 eggs
    butter for frying
    salt and pepper to taste
    paprika

You will need 6 small, lightly greased (7- to 8-inch) skillets. Fry 1 ham slice in each; cut ham in half, push to side of pan, add a little butter, and break in 2 eggs. Cook until whites have set. Sprinkle with salt, pepper, and paprika. Serve in the pan.

NOTE: Small breadboards are an easy answer to "how to serve," and they substitute nicely as plates for this outdoor meal.

* Recipe in this book.

HOME-FRIED POTATOES
SERVES SIX

    6 tablespoons butter
    3 cups diced cooked potatoes
    salt and pepper to taste

Melt butter in large skillet, add potatoes, and sprinkle lightly with salt and pepper. Stir until potatoes are well blended with butter. Press with spatula to smooth down; cook until bottom is well browned. Add remaining butter, loosen edges with spatula, turn, and brown other side.

Easy Buffet for Eight

Fresh Fruit Compote with Kirsch*
Broiled Bacon Rolls
Scrambled Eggs with Chives
Baked Tomatoes*
Jam- and Butter-Filled Rolls (Heated)
Coffee

BROILED BACON ROLLS

    2 cups soft bread crumbs
    2 tablespoons grated onion
    2 tablespoons finely chopped green pepper
    1 egg yolk, slightly beaten
    salt and coarse-ground black pepper to taste
    16 slices Irish bacon

Combine bread crumbs, onion, and green pepper in mixing bowl. Stir in egg yolk. Mix to a smooth paste. (Add a little water if needed to achieve desired consistency.) Season with salt (amount depends on saltiness of bacon) and pepper.

* Recipe in this book.

102

Place a teaspoon of the mixture on each slice of bacon and roll bacon loosely around filling. Secure with a toothpick. Broil, turning frequently, under medium flame, until bacon is crisp on all sides.

Saratoga Race Day Breakfast

Ramos Gin Fizz*
Well-Chilled Compote of Fresh Figs,
Sliced Bananas, and Fresh Apricot Halves
(Sprinkled with Lime Juice and
Confectioners' Sugar)
Baked Eggs in Béchamel Sauce
Broiled, Bacon-wrapped Chicken Livers
Sweet Potato Chips
Hot Biscuits*   Blueberry Muffins*
Butter Balls   Strawberry Jam
Hot Coffee   Morning Iced Coffee*

BAKED EGGS IN BÉCHAMEL SAUCE
SERVES SIX

- 2 ounces chopped lean veal
- 5 tablespoons butter
- 1 small chopped onion
- 1 teaspoon salt
- ¼ teaspoon white pepper
- nutmeg
- 1 bay leaf
- 1 sprig fresh thyme or pinch of thyme leaves
- 2 tablespoons flour
- 2 cups milk
- 12 eggs
- 2 tablespoons grated Gruyère cheese

* Recipe in this book.

Sauté the veal in 3 tablespoons butter until no longer pink. Add the onion and cook, stirring, until limp but not brown; season with salt and pepper plus a sprinkling of nutmeg. Add bay leaf and thyme, blend, and remove from heat. Melt remaining butter in top half of double boiler, stir in the flour; when bubbly, add milk and stir over low heat until smooth. Blend in the veal mixture and place over barely simmering water. Cook, stirring frequently, for 45 minutes to 1 hour. Strain the sauce through a fine sieve. If not used at once, dot surface with tiny slivers of butter to keep film from forming on surface. Cover and refrigerate until ready to reheat.

Butter 6 individual ramekins, spoon enough heated sauce into each to cover bottom of dish. Break in 2 eggs; cover with more sauce. Bake in moderate (350°F.) oven for 10 to 12 minutes or until egg whites have set. Sprinkle surface with grated cheese and place under hot broiler to brown. Serve at once.

BROILED, BACON-WRAPPED CHICKEN LIVERS
SERVES SIX

    12 chicken livers
    12 slices of bacon, cut in half

Halve each liver, wrap in bacon slice. Broil under medium flame, turning occasionally, until bacon is crisp on all sides.

SWEET POTATO CHIPS

    4 large sweet potatoes
    ice water
    oil for frying
    salt or confectioners' sugar

Peel sweet potatoes. Slice crosswise into very thin strips. Place in ice water to cover for 2 to 3 hours. Drain and pat dry. Fry in deep hot fat (375°F.) until crisp. Drain on paper toweling. Sprinkle with salt or confectioners' sugar. If prepared before serving time, place on brown paper (a large torn-open paper bag does nicely) in a "just warm" oven; they will remain crisp an hour or even a little longer.

Sunday Party Brunch

Orange Blossoms*
Milk Punch in Icy-Cold Pottery Mugs*
Thin-sliced Honeydew Melon
with Fresh Lime Juice and Chopped Mint
Baked Eggs Provençale
Bacon Curls   Link Sausage
Chicken Hash Served in a Chafing Dish
Hot Biscuits*
Muffins*
Coffee   Café au Lait*

BAKED EGGS PROVENCALE
SERVES SIX

2 large green peppers
1 small eggplant
2 tablespoons olive oil
2 tablespoons butter
1 clove garlic
6 eggs
1 cup prepared tomato sauce
chopped parsley

* Recipe in this book.

Cut 6 large rings, about ¼ inch thick, from the green peppers and discard seeds (chop remaining peppers, place in plastic bag, refrigerate for future use). Boil pepper rings in water for 5 to 10 minutes or until crisp-tender. Drain, set aside. Peel eggplant, cut into 6 slices, discard end pieces, and trim each piece to approximately the same size. Heat olive oil and butter with garlic in heavy skillet; discard garlic. Fry eggplant slices until tender, turning once. Remove with slotted spatula and place in single layer in lightly buttered, shallow oven-proof dish. Place a pepper ring in center of each slice. Gently break 1 egg into each pepper ring. Pour tomato sauce over and around eggs. Dot yolks with slivers of butter, and sprinkle with parsley. Bake at 350°F. approximately 15 minutes, or until whites are set. Serve from same dish.

CHICKEN HASH
SERVES SIX

3 tablespoons butter
2 tablespoons flour
2 cups milk
1 cup cream
salt and pepper to taste
2 egg yolks, beaten
4 cups diced cooked chicken
½ cup chopped blanched almonds
¼ cup chopped sweet pimiento
2 tablespoons dry sherry

Melt the butter in a heavy saucepan, stir in the flour; when bubbly add the milk and cream. Cook over very low heat, stirring frequently, until sauce begins to thicken. Remove from heat and add salt and pepper to taste. Beat in egg yolks, then add chicken, almonds, pimiento, and sherry. Pour into chafing dish or keep warm over low flame; dot surface with tiny slivers of butter; set aside until time to serve. Reheat in chafing dish and serve.

New Year's Day Buffet

Broiled Grapefruit
Eggs Benedict Gourmet
Honey Pecan Sticky Buns*
Coffee   Capuccino*

EGGS BENEDICT GOURMET
SERVES SIX

6 slices tomato
2 tablespoons butter
6 slices bread
anchovy butter (see p. 96)
6 thick slices Canadian bacon
6 poached eggs
blender Hollandaise sauce (see p. 108)
2 tablespoons parsley

Sauté tomato slices in butter for 2 minutes on each side. Trim crust from bread, cut into rounds slightly larger than Canadian bacon slices. Toast lightly. Spread with anchovy butter. Top with Canadian bacon, then tomato slice, then poached egg. Cover with blender Hollandaise sauce. Sprinkle with parsley and serve.

* Recipe in this book.

BLENDER HOLLANDAISE SAUCE

½ cup butter
3 egg yolks
2 tablespoons lemon juice
dash of cayenne pepper
¼ teaspoon salt

Heat butter in saucepan. Put remaining ingredients in electric blender. Run blender at low speed for 5 seconds. Reset for another 5 seconds at low speed; pour in butter in a steady slow stream. Reset and run on high speed for 2 seconds. Use immediately.

Skiers' Brunch

Choice of Bloody or Bloodless Marys*
Country-Fried Eggs
Southern-Fried Grits
Maple Syrup
Whole Baked Canadian Bacon
Coffee   Tea

COUNTRY-FRIED EGGS
SERVES SIX

6 to 12 eggs
butter
bacon grease
chopped chives
herb vinegar

Fry eggs, 1 or 2 per person depending on appetite, in half butter, half bacon grease (see basic egg instructions). When whites have almost set, sprinkle chives over yolks and add

* Recipe in this book.

herb vinegar to grease in pan. Continue cooking until eggs are done to taste. Remove with slotted spoon.

SOUTHERN-FRIED GRITS
SERVES SIX

2 teaspoons salt
4½ cups water
1 cup white cornmeal (grits)
½ to ⅔ cup flour
2 eggs plus 2 tablespoons water, beaten
1 cup fine dry bread crumbs
oil and butter for frying

Add salt to water, and bring to boil in top half of double boiler. Slowly add cornmeal, stirring constantly. Cover, place over simmering water, and cook until thick and creamy (1½ to 2 hours). Stir occasionally. Pour cooked grits into long, shallow, well-greased pan. Refrigerate 8 hours or overnight. Cut into slices approximately ½ inch thick. Dip first in flour, then into the beaten egg and water, and finally roll in bread crumbs. Fry in half butter, half oil over medium heat until crisp and well browned, turning once. Serve with maple syrup.

WHOLE BAKED CANADIAN BACON
SERVES SIX

2- to 2½-pound piece Canadian bacon
8 to 10 whole cloves
½ cup apple cider
½ cup brown sugar
½ teaspoon dry mustard

Place bacon, fat side up, on rack in roasting pan; stick cloves into surface and pour apple cider over it. Bake at 350°F. for

15 minutes. Combine sugar, mustard, and enough of the cider from pan to make a smooth paste. Spread over surface of bacon. Bake 45 minutes to 1 hour. Baste frequently. Place on serving platter, slice at the table.

Wedding Breakfast

Fresh Fruit Compote with Frozen Champagne*
Creamed Sweetbreads and Chicken
Served in a Chafing Dish
Patty Shells
Cold Baked Virginia Ham
Hot Buttered Parker House Rolls
Guava Jelly
Rolled Watercress Sandwiches
Wedding Cake
Champagne
Coffee   Tea

CREAMED SWEETBREADS AND CHICKEN
SERVES TWELVE

6 pairs sweetbreads
salt
2 tablespoons lemon juice
3 cups diced cooked chicken
sauce (see p. 111)
½ cup sliced fresh mushrooms
½ cup sliced ripe olives
¼ cup chopped sweet pimientos
¼ cup dry sherry

Soak the sweetbreads in ice water for 1 hour. Cook in boiling salted water with lemon juice for 20 minutes. Plunge into ice water. Remove and discard tubes and membranes. Slice into

* Recipe in this book.

2-inch pieces. Combine with chicken, sauce, mushrooms, olives, and pimientos. Heat thoroughly but do not allow to boil. Stir in sherry, transfer to chafing dish. Keep warm over very low flame until ready to serve. Spoon onto patty shells.

SAUCE

    4 tablespoons butter
    1 small onion, chopped
    4 tablespoons flour
    3 cups milk
    1 cup chicken stock
    1 teaspoon salt (less if chicken stock is salty)
    1 egg yolk
    ¼ cup dry sherry

Heat butter in large heavy saucepan, add onion, and cook over low heat until limp but not brown. Stir in flour, blend thoroughly; slowly add milk and chicken stock, stirring until well blended. Cook until sauce begins to thicken (keep heat low); add salt. Remove from heat, stir in egg yolk (a wire whisk is best for this job) and sherry. Dot surface of sauce with tiny slivers of butter. Set aside or refrigerate, covered, until ready to reheat and use.

BAKED VIRGINIA HAM

    1 10- to 12-pound country-style smoked Virginia ham
    1 tablespoon dry mustard
    2 tablespoons brandy
    1 cup light brown sugar
    1 tablespoon flour
    cloves
    1 cup pineapple juice

Soak ham overnight in water to cover. Drain. Place, fat side up, on rack in a roasting pan (one with a tight-fitting cover). Pour water into bottom of pan to a depth of about 2 inches. Cover and roast at 350°F., allowing 30 minutes to the pound. For last 30 minutes, remove from oven. Cut off rind and excess fat, except for collar of rind around shank bone. Make a thick paste of the mustard, brandy, sugar, and flour (adding a little additional flour if needed). Cover surface of ham with this mixture. Stud with cloves. Add pineapple juice to pan and return to oven. Baste frequently with pan juice. For last 15 minutes, increase heat to 425°F. to brown ham. Remove to serving platter and allow to cool 30 minutes or more before cutting. Serve hot or cold.

ROLLED WATERCRESS SANDWICHES
MAKES THIRTY-FIVE TO FORTY SMALL SANDWICHES

    1 loaf very fresh white bread, sliced
    ½ pound soft butter (at room temperature)
    1 cup chopped watercress

Remove crust from bread. Place slices on dampened paper toweling. Roll flat with rolling pin. Spread with butter. Cover butter with watercress. Roll up, jelly-roll fashion, and cut each roll in half. Store, wrapped in lightly dampened cloth, in refrigerator until ready to serve. Or place, not touching, on flat tray and freeze until firm. Wrap in foil and store in freezer.

Menus

🌞
Well-Chilled Stewed Prunes and Banana Slices
Sprinkled with Fresh Lemon Juice
Scrambled Eggs with Oysters
à la Louisiane*
"Quick Delivery" Bread*
Strawberry Jam

🌞
Apple Frappé*
Splendiferous Eggs*
Paper-Thin Slices of Smoked Salmon
French-Style Melba Toast
Sweet Butter

🌞
Margaritas*
Huevos Rancheros*
Hot Garlic Bread
Guava Shells

*Recipe in this book.

🌞

Tomato Juice on the Rocks "Spiked" with
Fresh Lime Juice and Chopped Parsley
Oeufs sur le Plat Lorraine*
Fresh Pineapple Slices
Heated Crusty Hard Rolls   Butter

☀

Vodka Orange Juice over Crushed Ice
(One Part Vodka to Five Parts Orange Juice)
Baked Eggs in Tomato Shells*
Hashed Brown Potatoes
Sausage Patties
Louisiana Corn Bread*
Apple Jelly

☀

Sliced Fresh Pineapple
and Honeydew Melon Wedges
Omelet Parmentier*
Broiled Canadian Bacon
Marmalade
French Bread, Buttered and Toasted
Café au Lait*

☀

Fresh Figs with Cream
Puffy Virginia Ham Omelet*
Grilled Tomato Slices
Corn Bread Sticks
Tart Jelly

☀

Cantaloupe Halves Filled with Raspberries
Omelet Clamart*
Little Link Sausages
Buttered Toast   Strawberry Jam

* Recipe in this book.

Blueberries with Cream
Omelet aux Croûtons*
Sausage Patties
Split and Toasted Hard Rolls

☼

Poached Apples with Thick Cream*
Omelet au Fromage Grand-Mère*
Bacon Biscuits*
Tart Jelly

☼

Well-Chilled V-8 Juice
Ham Soufflé in Green Peppers*
Pickled Peaches
Toasted English Muffins with Cream Cheese

☼

Fresh Pineapple Slices
Small Bunches of Grapes
Vegetable Soufflé Ring with Chipped Beef
in Sherried Cream Sauce*
Toasted Sesame-Seed French Bread
Cottage Cheese   Orange Marmalade

☼

Fresh Figs
Shrimp Soufflé New Orleans*
Heated French Rolls   Sweet Butter
Watermelon Rind Preserves

☼

Fresh Orange Juice and Canned Papaya Juice,
Half 'n' Half
Buttermilk Griddle Cakes*
Maple Syrup   Butter
Double-Thick Slices of Broiled Bacon

* Recipe in this book.

☼

Well-Chilled Tomato Juice
Seasoned with a Squeeze of Fresh Lemon
Applesauce Pancakes Deluxe*
Warm Applesauce   Butter
Grilled Vienna Sausages

☀

Well-Chilled Compote
of Fresh Orange Sections, Sliced Bananas,
and Fresh Pineapple Chunks
Crêpes Dusted with Confectioners' Sugar*
Baked Virginia Ham, Sliced Paper-Thin
and Sautéed in Butter*

☀

Honeydew Melon Halves
Filled with Fresh Blackberries and
Topped with Sour Cream
Deep-Fried Fritters*
Lazy Susan of Assorted Jams
Bacon Curls and Spicy Link Sausages

☀

Well-Chilled Tangerine Juice
Broiled Kippers*
Potato Balls with Parsley Butter
Buttered, Oven-Toasted Country-Style
White Bread
Marmalade   Greengage Jam

☀

Fresh Cantaloupe and Honeydew Melon
Trout Meunière*
Oven-Baked Potato Slices*
Corn Muffins*
Butter Balls   Comb Honey

* Recipe in this book.

116

Ugli Fruit
Broiled Shad Roe Beurre Noir*
Crisp Bacon   Scrambled Eggs*
Buttered Rye Toast
Pear Conserve

☀

Brown Sugar-Sprinkled Grapefruit Halves
Haddock Fillets in Oatmeal*
Country-Fried Potatoes*
Brown Bread   Sweet Butter
Homemade Applesauce

☀

Sliced Fresh Pineapple
Sautéed Smelts with Deviled Butter Sauce*
Potato Sticks
Popovers*   Apricot Jam

☀

Sliced Oranges
Minted Baked Apples with Cream*
Kedgeree*
Grilled Bacon and Kidneys
Black Treacle Scones*
Toast
Quince Jelly   Strawberry Jam
English Breakfast Tea*

☀

Peaches with Strawberry Purée*
Parsley Codfish Cakes*
Stewed Tomatoes
Muffins
Currant Jelly   Cottage Cheese

* Recipe in this book.

☀

Index

119